policy analysis and education series

DALE MANN, GENERAL EDITOR

Delivering
Educational
Service

Urban Schools
and Schooling Policy

David Goodwin
National Institute of Education

Teachers College Press
Teachers College, Columbia University
New York

Library of Congress Cataloging in Publication Data

Goodwin, David
    Delivering educational service.

    Bibliography: p.
    Includes index.
    1. Education, Urban—United States. 2. School
management and organization—United States. I. Title.
LC5131.G66   370.19′348′0973   76-54166
ISBN 0-8077-2507-2 pbk.

Manufactured in the United States of America

Designed by Angela Foote

To my son Matthew

General Editor's Introduction

Since Mark Hopkins made his remark about the best educational system being a log with the teacher on one end and the student on the other, we have piled a great many things on and around that basic teaching-learning system. Supervisors, administrators, teams, house plans, acres of new curricula have been invented and justified as ways to improve learning. As David Goodwin demonstrates in this book, their impact is debatable. What is not debatable is that reformers and analysts have tended to concentrate their attention on almost every part of the system except the teachers themselves. It has been technically and (especially) politically more feasible to hope to improve schools by having improved almost everything but the teacher. Thus we have seen efforts to "teacher-proof" the curriculum, to supplant the teacher, and to condition the teacher's behavior by changing physical or organizational artifacts.

But, as most leaders have always known and as policy analysts are now learning, the final arbiter of improvement is the teacher who will decide what—if anything—is to be done. As President, John Kennedy struggled to get American missles removed from Turkey so that the Russians would not have a gratuitous bargaining counter in case of a nuclear confrontation. The high status, the great power of the Office of the President, and the clarity of the policy instructions came to naught when they weren't implemented by the Army. The message is clear—without the delivery level, there is no policy.

Thus, Goodwin's searching analysis of teachers as service deliverers can provide some important insight for policy makers. While it may not make any difference how the Army's motor pool feels about the missles they transport, it makes a lot of difference how teachers feel about the children in their classes, the schools in which they work, and the neighborhoods where the schools are located. Teacher attitudes are the central focus of this book and Goodwin links those attitudes toward the socio-political reality of schooling. Schools acquire their micro-political vitality courtesy of the inexorable laws of scarcity. There is never enough useful pedagogy, time, or goodwill to satisfy all the demands made on schools. Thus the school person's political problem is how to distribute the benefits of teaching. That decision helps determine who will benefit and who will not benefit from the school. Goodwin examines variations in teachers' attitudes toward the different groups they must satisfy— parents, other teachers, administrative subordinates, and children. He shows how the organizational surround shapes teacher attitudes, and how those attitudes vary by the social class of the student and by the personal and professional characteristics of the teachers.

Contemporary school reformers have often concentrated their attacks on the bureaucratic nature of schooling—an improvement, by the way, brought to education by an earlier group of reformers. But, while it has been easy to rail against petty regulations and petty behaviors, most of those attacks have been fueled by ideology and anecdote, not by data. How do teachers regard the rule structure of their schools? Are all rules the same? Do teachers of all sorts regard the schooling bureaucracy the same way? Is it true that ghetto schools have a disproportionate number of the least trained, least experienced teachers? Where students are poor and black, are most of their teachers white and middle class? How, in fact, does bureaucracy affect the delivery of services? The contemporary empirical literature on these subjects is beginning to teach another lesson about bureaucracy. In the interstices of offices, and rules, and channels, manuals, and operating procedures individuals can find or create great freedom of maneuver, In a curious paradox, discretion may be as much a product of bureaucracy as paralysis. Given the inevitability of bureaucracy, Goodwin's examination of this topic is important and topical.

The final aspect commending this book to an audience of policy makers is not in its analysis, but in current events about teachers. By their organization, by their growing political influence in the traditional community and national arenas; and by their clout at the bargaining table, teachers are major figures in the policy arena. That corporate role is a relatively recent phenomenon. The role examined in this book stresses the determination of policy by the aggregation of individual decisions at the delivery level. The importance of teachers as a focus for policy analysis is thus doubly important.

Dale Mann
New York City

Preface

The principal aim of this book is to describe patterns of school organization and to examine their consequences for teacher performance. Much current rhetoric about school reform is based on assumptions for which evidence is scanty. This study examines relevant data in an effort to verify or refute some of these assumptions. Although the focus is on elementary schools, the reader will no doubt observe some basic similarities about school life at all educational levels.

Research on school politics has traditionally focused on high level decision-makers and dramatic school conflicts. As a result, researchers are better able to describe how decisions are made than to trace their impact on everyday classroom behavior. Furthermore, urban school systems have been popularly portrayed as large bureaucracies with tight control exercised by top level decision-makers. School reformers have claimed, perhaps erroneously, that such bureaucratic organization breeds apathy, arrogance toward clients, and rigid, ritualistic behavior on the part of school officials. Lastly, educational policies have often failed because of the gap between adoption and successful implementation of innovative programs and practices.

Strategies for innovation, it is argued, fall short because they typically fail to consider the necessary conditions for implementation beyond district headquarters. Implementation plans, where they exist, are often oblivious to organizational realities. Such realities are ones in which schools are increasingly beset with noneducational responsibilities, for which classroom teachers must exercise considerable discretion in balancing competing roles while seeking to preserve challenged authority. In stark contrast, more theoretical conceptions view school organization as predominantly bureaucratic, in which authority is hierarchically ordered, teacher roles are clearly defined, and discretional behavior is highly limited. Such a view, it is argued, contains serious distortions, leads to faulty conclusions about the suitability of various widely considered school reforms, and diminishes the chances that innovative educational ideas, whatever their merits, may be successfully translated into actual practice.

This book has been written for two main audiences: school personnel—teachers and prospective teachers, administrators, and policy-makers—who work on a daily basis with the problems of providing education, often in difficult organizational settings; and social scientists, who view the study of schools as a barometer of government service in an urban society.

There are many people whose interests and intellect played a large role throughout this study. Matthew Crenson and Francis Rourke of The Johns Hopkins University freely gave their wise counsel in helping me grapple with problems of research design and conceptualization. James Nathanson of Case Western Reserve University suffered my methodological naïveté, patiently answering questions at all times of the day and night. Dale Mann of Teachers College, Columbia University, provided valuable substantive and editorial comments. Constance Goddard and Janet Simons, editors at Teachers College Press, helped improve the final manuscript at a time when I had long lost the desire to do so. Thanks are due my colleagues at the National Institute of Education for their encouragement; the views expressed in the book are, however, mine alone, and are not necessarily those of my associates or of the N.I.E. I also want to thank Sharon Powell, who typed an early version of the manuscript and thereby shaped it into legible appearance. Greatest thanks go to those teachers, principals, and other administrators who participated in the study.

Finally, I would like to thank my parents, Ernest and Pearl, and my wife, Matou, for supporting my efforts in obvious and subtle ways.

David Goodwin
Washington, D. C.

Contents

Tables

Delivering Educational Service

I

The Politics
of Teacher Behavior

In recent years, urban institutions have been the battlegrounds for intense rhetorical and at times physical violence. Perhaps because of their intimate connection with the daily lives of most citizens, public schools have experienced more than their share of unrest. One arena of conflict has been at the level of system-wide policy-making—over such complex issues as community control, desegregation, budgets, selection of superintendents and school boards, school construction and taxes, union recognition, personnel recruitment and tenure. These areas of conflict, in which decisions are made at the top of the school system hierarchy, do not exhaust, however, the range of school-community conflict, or the ways in which urban institutions intersect the lives of city residents.

Another face of urban conflict is identified in the concept of street-level bureaucracy,[1] where teachers and their immediate clients (pupils and parents) frequently seem frustrated, aggressive, and hostile in their dealings with one another. Teacher-client relations need not, of course, be characterized by conflict. More typical patterns involve cooperation, compliance or, at the least, indifference. Nevertheless, the way in which people perceive the delivery of educational services, and in large measure what those services actually are, is the product of these daily face-to-face encounters.

Although public discussion of school affairs commonly arises when major conflicts, key decisions, changes in leadership, or other events receive the focus of media coverage, this represents only a fraction of the continuous relationship between schools and their constituents. Likewise, concentration of scholarly study upon such system-wide issues as school board elections, desegregation battles, and bond issues fails to capture a dimension of school politics, which is largely routine and unobserved by individuals other than the immediate participants. The delivery of educational services in schools and classrooms offers an opportunity for citizens to view local government as it affects their daily lives.

Public perceptions of schools are largely derived from three sources: (1) childhood and adolescent experiences that predispose individuals, as adults, to interact with and observe school officials in a particular manner; (2) highly visible, dramatic but intermittent system-wide issues such as strikes, scandals, and school board elections; and (3) intimate long-term, recurrent, largely unobserved, and undramatic face-to-face associations between school officials and clientele. Such private face-to-face contacts between schools and constituents may, over time, shape still larger public views of the political process. They are also the focus of this book.

Even during periods of relative tranquility in the schools, political and educational processes are closely intertwined. Schools are typically expected to play an important role in economic and social mobility, foster allegiance to the political system, and transmit the society's most revered social and political values from one generation to the next. When school conflict occurs, public perception of school politics shifts away from the collective benefits of public education to the community as a whole, and focuses on the divisiveness associated with urban schools. Instead of compensating for social inequities—by opening the economic and political system to racial, ethnic, and economic minorities—schools are seen as cementing and broadening existing social inequalities—by conferring benefits upon some and neglecting others. For many city residents, the experience of dealing with school officials, either as students or as parents, represents a visible and direct symbol of government unresponsiveness to their needs and unfairness in the distribution of valued services.

With the decline of old party machines, government bureaucracies have assumed basic responsibility for the delivery of essential public services. Where welfare, legal assistance, and family counseling were once the province of neighborhood ward captains, these functions have been largely taken over by various public agencies. It is perhaps inevitable, therefore, that urban bureaucracies would appear to many as exercising their powers in ways similar to machines—conferring benefits upon some groups and withholding them from others. Nevertheless, if public perceptions of arbitrariness, favoritism, bias, and unequal treatment are accurate, they represent departures from the ethic that brought about decline of machines—the desire for bureaucratic impartiality and professional delivery of vital public services.

Because teachers are basic components of any educational system, one way of viewing the allocation of educational resources in a school system is in terms of the important differences among its teachers. Teacher decisions regarding curriculum, instructional materials, and student discipline represent small but cumulatively significant examples of the way in which teachers control a vital dimension in the flow of educational resources to students. This view regards teachers and educational administrators as part of the political process. Like elected officials or the traditional party machine, their decisions and behavior significantly influence the nature of government services.

This perspective also illustrates the way in which more general conceptions of public administration have changed. Although traditional theories clearly distinguish politics and public administration, contemporary students increasingly regard administrative discretion as a prominent aspect of policy-making. Traditional theorists argue that the goals of government are established by elected or appointed political officials—the mayor, president, or legislators—although administrative underlings are limited to the achievement of objectives. As stated by Woodrow Wilson: "The broad plans of governmental action are not administrative; the detailed execution of such plans is administrative."[2]

With the growth of public bureaucracies has come abundant evidence, however, that administrative discretion extends beyond the implementation of decisions to the very formulation of public policy. Francis Rourke notes that "the scope of this administrative discretion is vast with respect to both everyday decisions of government agencies and the major innovative trend-setting decisions of organizational life."[3] The exercise of bureaucratic discretion over routine, everyday matters is as significant for the individuals involved as is prior administrative "shaping" of major policies and programs.

The purpose of this book is to examine classroom attitudes of teachers that bear upon the daily delivery of educational services and the implication of these attitudes for policy-makers. The attitudes considered are those toward school clients (pupils and parents), the principal, school innovation, parental participation in school decision-making, and the use of routines in classroom management. The study examines the way in which these attitudes are affected by (a) bureaucratic school organization, (b) the social class and educational attributes of students, and (c) individual personal and professional characteristics of teachers. Lastly, the study considers ways in which the configuration of teacher attitudes affects national and local strategies for implementing new educational ideas and programs. Some of the questions addressed follow.

1. Do characteristics of the student body such as race and income of families affect the attitudes of teachers? Are students in schools that are predominantly poor and black, with low student achievement rates and high truancy, more likely to receive inferior treatment from their teachers than those in middle-income, white schools?

Case studies and anecdotal accounts of schools are replete with horror stories about social class and racial inequality. Ray Rist's study of St. Louis schools concluded that

> throughout the various levels of the St. Louis educational system we found commonly shared assumptions about how things really are. The basic tenets may be summarized as follows: middle-class students can learn, lower-class students cannot; white schools are good, black schools are bad; control is necessary, freedom is anarchy; violence works, persuasion does not; teachers can save a few but will lose many; the school tries, the home will not; and finally, only the naive would dispute these beliefs, as the wise know. The outcome of this set of attitudes, assumptions and values is that the school as an institution sustains, in a myriad of ways, the inequalities with which children come to school.[4]

Despite such sobering assessments, policy-makers have scanty reliable information to guide them in redressing school inequality. The Coleman Report, for example, concluded that tangible school resources and teacher ability are less significant predictors of student achievement than is the socioeconomic composition of the student body.[5] This study will examine some of the educational resources that are often said to distinguish good from bad, rich from poor, and black from white schools— teacher credentials, teaching experience, social origins, and perhaps most important, attitudes of teachers toward students, parents, and other aspects of the teaching role.

2. Do administrative practices have any relationship to the way in which teachers handle their classroom responsibilities on a daily basis? Are teachers in schools organized along the lines of bureaucratic principles (formal rules for teacher behavior) more likely than teachers in non-

*bureaucratic schools to express disdainful attitudes toward pupils, par-
ents, and principal, resist innovation and parental participation, and
attempt to routinize the classroom behavior of students?*

The literature on school politics and administration contains frequent
reference to the effects of school bureaucracy. David Rogers has characterized the New York City school system as "typical of what social scientists call a sick bureaucracy—a term for organizations whose traditions,
structure and operations subvert their stated missions and prevent any
flexible accommodation to changing client demands."[6] Schools are commonly termed bureaucratic as a synonym for settings that thwart teacher
creativity, reward conformity, reduce teachers to compulsive rule follow-
ers, and increase insulation from clients.

Tales of petty bureaucratic rituals that have long outlived their intended purpose are grist for school critics. Although popular jargon
equates bureaucracy with ineptitude, there has been little effort to view
school bureaucracy as a form of organization objectively divorced from its
presumed negative consequences. This study measures the extent to
which teaching tasks are truly specified by bureaucratic rules, and
whether such rules contribute to the charactistics of a "sick" bureaucracy.

3. *What are the attributes of the principal, student body, and faculty
that affect patterns of organizational control over teachers? In short, if
bureaucracy is the basis of school organization, what pupil, teacher, and
other school factors give rise to this pattern?*

4. *Are the social attributes of teachers, such as race, age, and sex,
significant factors related to teacher attitudes? Do professional qualities,
such as education, teaching experience, and tenure, have any bearing
upon teacher attitudes?*

5. *How do interpersonal and organizational relationships among key
parties in schools facilitate or hamper policies designed to alter school
practices? Assuming that sound education requires some stability in the
relationship among teachers, administrators, and clients, how does programmatic and organizational change get accommodated?*

Alternate Approaches to the
Study of School Politics

Some of the central ideas in this study derive from themes discussed by
community power theorists. One school of thought, represented by Floyd

Hunter and C. Wright Mills,[7] has emphasized the dominant influence of social and economic elites upon major decisions in all areas of public life. They argue that a small handful of upper-class individuals controls the political leadership and receives more than their fair share of government benefits. As one of the major institutions in our society, school systems are pictured as the handmaidens of privileged elites. School boards comprise those who represent the interests of business, labor, and "high" society; curriculum is characterized by an abiding reverence for the status quo. These studies have been criticized, however, for not focusing upon specific school decisions and institutions, and for assuming that the distribution of public services mirrors the desires of private elites.[8]

Those who have found a pluralist interpretation to be more persuasive, such as Robert Dahl, Wallace Sayre, and Herbert Kaufman, consider public education a primary function of local government, and therefore likely to provide important clues to the distribution of power and rewards. In their respective studies of New Haven[9] and New York City,[10] they emphasize the diversity of interests and influence represented in the decision-making process. They also suggest the large capacity for insulation, autonomy, and independence enjoyed by school officials. This insulation is consistent with Lowi's assertion that the locus of local political power has shifted from the party machine to the major urban bureaucracies—education, police, housing, and welfare.[11]

Although these studies have not focused upon teachers per se, their findings suggest a perspective from which to view this inquiry. The political process allocates benefits unevenly among groups and individuals: by exercising discretion to withold, dispense, or concentrate educational services, school personnel allocate important rewards. Although the school system and its personnel may enjoy a large measure of independence from the control of partisan electoral politics, the exercise of administrative and professional discretion over routine decisions plays an important role in the distribution of valued educational benefits. By examining the interrelationship between school bureaucracy, clientele characteristics, and teacher attributes, this study will suggest some of the factors that shape these allocations on a daily basis.

Several studies that focus explicitly on school politics emphasize the elitist nature of decision-making. In his study of desegregation, Crain suggests that school boards enjoy a large degree of autonomy from civil rights and conservative pressure groups.[12] Roger's study of New York City integration battles argues that bickering and competition among civil rights groups left school leaders with considerable latitude to avoid effective desegregation.[13] Gittell suggests that, by controlling bureaucratic rules, a narrow elite of education professionals is able to dominate major decisions regarding choice of superintendent, budgets, and curriculum.[14] Instead of simply examining the socioeconomic group membership of decision-makers (as in Floyd Hunter's study of community power in Atlanta), more recent work has focused on questions of bureaucratic elitism, organizational structure, authority, and control.

Although they usefully identify the issues of social class and bureaucratic organization, the studies mentioned have a variety of shortcomings. From this study's point of view, perhaps their greatest weakness is the limited manner in which school organizations are studied. By focusing exclusively on school system leaders (as elites or agents of ruling groups), they present a partial and perhaps biased view of how schools operate in conferring and withholding rewards on a daily basis. These studies fail to consider the role of subordinates, notably teachers, in the delivery of educational services.

James Q. Wilson has suggested that the police and other urban institutions are characterized by increasing discretion over the performance of daily tasks at the bottom of the organization hierarchy.[15] The exercise of discretion occurs in situations where formal rules and professional norms are absent, or provide contradictory and ambiguous guides to appropriate behavior. Consequently, policemen on the beat make many decisions on the basis of subjective judgments and experience in face-to-face relations with the public. Wilson suggests that a considerable gap exists between the day-to-day behavior of police officers and the official decisions made at police headquarters. The inevitable discretion left to individual officers gives rise to considerable variation in the way laws are enforced and order is maintained; consequently, there are distinctly different views of police behavior among segments of the urban community.

The exercise of discretion is an important component of teacher behavior as well. Charles Bidwell contrasts the bureaucratic operation of schools according to rules and procedures with their structural looseness (which stems from their geographic disperson), variability among their students, and the self-contained nature of classrooms.[16] He distinguishes between the discretion of teachers to determine how services are to be provided on a daily basis, and the uniformity and routinization of decisions regarding recruitment, promotion, and compensation. C. Wayne Gordon argues that the penetration of student society and values into the classroom forces teachers to rely on their personality and affective interaction with students, rather than on uniform standards of official authority.[17] The daily interaction among students and teachers gives rise to face-to-face relationships, which may supplant formal, uniform, institutional bases of behavior. Consequently, administrative hierarchy, formal authority, and leadership factors have a limited capacity to alter the manner in which teachers deal with students in the classroom.

The work of Wilson, Bidwell, Gordon, and others, suggests that studies focusing on decisions of organization leaders may obscure the impact of teacher discretion on the delivery of educational services. In general, organizations in which work is not structured around technology tend to formalize and centralize decisions about employment, but let daily activities be guided by a high level of discretion. Whereas salaries, promotions, and tenure decisions are governed by clear requirements and procedures, much of what goes on in the classroom—pedagogical techniques, student discipline, and discussions with parents—involves the exercise of considerable teacher judgment.

Studies of school politics that emphasize decisions regarding desegregation, budgets, recruitment, curriculum, and the like, therefore present only a partial perspective of school politics. Their emphasis on homogeneity of leadership and centralized control over urban schools could represent the consequence of bias in the issues chosen for study. Indeed, decisions in such areas as desegregation, budgets, and selection of superintendents may have been selected for study precisely because they require central decisions, are made with written and public records, and are therefore most visible to the researcher.

In extending the notion of organizational autonomy, Lipsky constructed his theory of street-level bureaucracy.[18] He emphasizes the chaotic consequences that limited organizational authority, ambiguous role expectations, and the exercise of discretion have for encounters between urban officials and citizens. He argues that concentration on formal decisions at the highest levels of public bureaucracy obscures the reality of daily interaction with urban residents. Previous studies of school-system politics have been limited by their predominant concern with organizational and social elites. Although the present work is similarly woven around the concepts of social class and bureaucracy, it emphasizes their effect on day-to-day relations between teachers and clients.

There are significant policy implications that flow from this perspective. Educational reform is fraught with examples of well-conceived innovations that are slowly, if ever, actually accepted in local schools. More than ever before, we are painfully aware of the gap between legislating reform at the national level and enacting changes in the classroom. By 1976, the annual federal investment in educational research and development exceeded $600 million.[19] In view of such substantial investment, federal policy-makers are continually challenged to develop better

THE POLITICS OF TEACHER BEHAVIOR

ways for school people to use the products of this research and development.

In other areas of education policy, the barriers to local implementation of new practices are of similar concern. In their study of Supreme Court decisions prohibiting school prayer, Dolbeare and Hammond examined the gap between national policy and actual practice at the local level.[20] In the five midwestern communities studied, the authors saw a pattern of community values, interest-group opposition, inertia, and lack of enforcement mechanisms that combined to perpetuate the unconstitutional practice of school prayer.

On the local level, numerous studies indicate the organizational, personal, and ideological barriers to implementation of innovations. Goodlad and Klein, for example, have noted that, despite professional support for innovations such as ungraded classes and team teaching, these innovations are difficult to implement.[21] Quite frequently, schools adopt new names for traditional practices; because the rhetoric of school innovation typically outpaces actual practice, it is frequently observed that "the more things change, the more they remain the same."

Models of Teacher Behavior

The literature on schools and urban politics contains several competing themes regarding the determinants of teacher behavior *vis-à-vis* clients. Each approach offers a different explanation for similar phenomena—the attitudes and behavior of teachers that communicate hostility toward clients, rigidity in classroom management, rejection of innovation, and resistance to parental participation in school decision-making; in short, attitudes that suggest a basis for client perceptions of mistreatment or educational indifference of teachers. These themes, or models, seek to explain teacher-client relationships in terms of such factors as social class, personal teacher attributes, the effects of school bureaucracy, and the demands of various teaching tasks.

The Social Class Model

The social class model emphasizes the impact of environmental variables on teacher behavior and role expectations. Characteristics of clientele such as race and economic status are prime ingredients determining inequalities in tangible school resources and the nature of school relationships between teachers and pupils. Many observers argue that social and educational inequality is perpetuated by a self-fulfilling prophecy in which teachers assume that lower-class children can't learn.[22] Attitudes communicated by teachers are translated, it is suggested, into lower expectations and subsequent achievement deficiencies on the part of poor, largely minority-group students.

Others suggest that teacher behavior in lower-class schools is conditioned by the nature of daily work problems in these schools; high rates of truancy and transiency among students, frequent discipline problems, and low achievement rates frustrate and demoralize faculty members. Some observers speak of a kind of cultural clash between the middle-class expectations of teachers and the values of students from poor families. They note that experienced teachers tend to transfer from inner-city to middle-class schools at the earliest opportunity. The result is an inequitable distribution of teaching skills, with the least experienced, frequently least competent, teachers in schools with predominantly poor, largely black or Spanish-speaking, enrollment.

Herriott and St. John's survey of urban schools found that teachers in lower-class schools were more likely than those in middle- and upper-class settings to seek transfers, express dissatisfaction with students and their job, and have low morale.[23] In addition, as judged by their school principal, such teachers were considered less likely to be receptive to new classroom methods, or interested in their pupils.

Michael Lipsky writes that street-level bureaucrats "have inherent difficulties in serving clienteles consisting predominantly of minority groups and other stigmatized individuals. Further, because of certain characteristic behavior patterns, they may be incapable of responding to pressure from client groups, and [their behavior] may be structured in such ways as to exacerbate the very conflicts which they otherwise declare interest in ameliorating."[24] Among the behavior patterns he cites are the simplification and routinization of behavior, the use of racial and social stereotypes, and a proprietary obsession with protecting authority. In short, the social class model suggests that teachers in schools with substantial proportions of lower-class, minority-group students, confronted with the educational problems that often characterize such schools, are likely to subordinate pedagogy to the custodial functions of teachers (through autocratic discipline), and strive to protect authority against potential threats posed by new organizational and decision-making practices (such as community control).

Not all the evidence suggests that ethnic and economic minorities are treated unfairly. In a study done for the National Advisory Commission on Civil Disorders, Peter Rossi interviewed teachers in urban ghetto schools. He found they expressed a general sensitivity toward the problems of racial inequality and poverty, and a view of "parents of their pupils as cooperative and supportive."[25]

The Teacher Attributes Model

A corollary of the social class model is the notion that individual teacher attributes explain much of the variation in teacher attitudes. Race and economic background of the teacher, for example, are thought to create the basis for cultural misunderstanding and conflict. White middle-class teachers in inner-city schools, it is alleged, may harbor racial or class biases, provide unsuitable role models, or fail to understand the needs and life styles of students in their classes. Herriott and St. John write:

> The middle-class family is said to be child-centered, future oriented, and interested in achievement and mobility. It teaches children to respect property and to value neatness, thrift, and punctuality. The lower-class family, on the other hand, is described as adult-centered, present oriented, and interested in enjoying life with family and peers. It teaches children to admire toughness, physical prowess, generosity and practicality. Since these values of the middle and lower class differ widely, there is, it is argued, a culture gap between teachers and pupils in most schools.[26]

In addition to race and economic background, teacher attributes such as sex and age are frequently said to influence teacher attitudes bearing upon performance in the classroom. Subsequent socialization and sorting out processes that occur through teacher training and job experience are further factors alleged to distinguish styles of teacher behavior and orientations toward students.

There is limited evidence to suggest that personal traits of teachers influence their classroom performances. In Ryan's study of teacher characteristics, older and more experienced teachers displayed less desirable classroom behavior than younger and inexperienced teachers.[27] In addition, at the elementary school level, men were deemed less responsible and businesslike in the classroom; they were more inclined, however, toward democratic classroom practices and child-centered philosophy, and were more emotionally stable than women. Charters examined the literature, however, and concluded that research has yet to establish a conclusive relationship between the personal attributes of teachers and their classroom behavior.[28]

Although evidence on the effects of teacher social background is at best skimpy, it contains some important implications for the political process. Political scientists often note the role of urban bureaucrats as a vehicle for social mobility among ethnic groups. In New York City, for example, police are historically Irish, firemen are Italian, and teachers are predominantly Jewish. Similarly, in New Haven, the growth of political influence among ethnic groups has marched hand in hand with employment opportunities in urban bureaucracies. To the extent that education of lower-class children is believed to suffer from a culture gap with middle-class educators, new teacher recruitment policies are likely to open school systems to employment of previously underrepresented ethnic groups. Efforts to redress the purported gap between middle-class school officials and lower-class students may necessitate hiring school personnel with racial, cultural, and social attributes similar to neighborhood residents.

The Bureaucratic Model

Instead of focusing upon socioeconomic attributes of teachers and their clients, the bureaucratic model stresses the importance of organizational rules in determining the contours of daily encounters between teachers, pupils, parents, and principal. Defining the salient characteristics of bureaucracy as the adherence to a system of formal rules and procedures for the performance of basic tasks, Robert Merton writes:

> adherence to the rules, originally conceived as a means, becomes transformed into ends-in-itself; there occurs the familiar process of displacement of goals whereby an instrumental value becomes a terminal value.... This emphasis, resulting from the displacement of the original goals, develops into rigidities and an inability to adjust readily. Formalism, even ritualism, ensues with an unchallenged insistence upon punctilious adherence to formalized procedures.[29]

James Anderson applied the bureaucratic model to a study of junior high school teachers in Baltimore and found that:

> The main control over the pursuit of its [the school's] objectives that the administration has at its disposal is the enforcement of rules and standards for teachers. Rules and standards then, determine the nature of the interaction between students and teachers, and thus determine the actual goals of the school to a far greater extent than does any particular allocation of time to the various school activities.

Anderson concluded that

> conflict in education, as in many other organizations, is between two bases of authority, the profession and the bureaucracy. Within the junior high school, the conflict between the professionals and bureaucrats is evident at all

levels.... When their expectations are frustrated ...teachers will abandon them for a bureaucratic orientation characterized by apathy, a rigid adherence to rules and regulations, an impersonal attitude toward students and a search for cues from administrators before making decisions. These unprofessional attitudes, though decried by school administrators, school boards, and the public are the result of bureaucratically structured school systems that foster and reward such behavior.[30]

Critics have charged that school bureaucracies are too large, too hierarchical, too impersonal, and, in a heterogeneous urban environment, too insulated from the educational needs of different clientele groups. Examples of petty bureaucratic rule conformity are legend: a student denied a high school diploma for missing one semester of physical education, rules that require teachers to complete specified curriculum units regardless of student ability to comprehend their content. School bureaucracy, its critics allege, substitutes a narrow conformity to rules for sound educational practice, deifies organizational needs while neglecting those of clients, and minimizes personal interaction with students and parents. This view of school bureaucracy imbeds many discussions of educational policy. Currently touted educational reforms, such as vouchers, community control, decentralization, performance contracting, and mastery learning, would theoretically curb the authority of school bureacracy to control educational practice.

The Task Model

The task model of teacher behavior emphasizes that the problem of getting the front line worker—teacher, housing inspector, police officer, or welfare worker—to "do the right thing" is intimately connected with the nature of functions performed. Institutional rules, formal expertise, and individual personalities are only partial determinants of behavior and attitudes on the job. In *Justice Without Trial*, Jerome Skolnick argues that the way policemen act may be determined more by "the duties police are called upon to perform" than by official rules and the quality of the policemen themselves.[31] Similarly, James Q. Wilson contrasts the nature of order maintenance and law enforcement tasks;[32] police are intimately involved with interpreting community values, for example, when they arrest disorderly drunks, enforce obscenity laws, or restrain unpopular public speakers. Wilson suggests that public perceptions of police bias, arbitrariness, and malfeasance stem from the kind of adaptive strategies police use to cope with demands posed by these tasks. As a result of experience on the job, the police develop a general cynicism characterized by distrust of the public, avoidance of responsibility, and attempts to minimize involvement with community residents. Wilson emphasizes that changes in formal rules, training, and recruitment may not have much effect in modifying this kind of behavior.

These police studies stress that expectations about appropriate role behavior stem from forces arising in the performance of basic tasks. Bryan Wilson, Amitai Etzioni, and others argue that teachers experience similar stress, insecurity, and role ambiguity because of the diffuse nature of the tasks they perform.[33] They contrast the affective, particularistic, value-laden nature of child socialization and discipline, with the specific, objective, secular quality of expertise needed in instruction. With the decline of child labor in factories and farms, much of the burden for child development has shifted from family and work settings to schools. In addition to basic instruction, teacher responsibilities have steadily grown to include therapy, guidance, health, and moral development. With expectations regarding teacher behavior extending beyond the bounds of definable, legitimate competence, it is alleged that teachers are frustrated in attempts to reach largely unattainable goals.

Studies of teacher behavior frequently fail to consider the diffuse and varied nature of teacher roles. By concentrating exclusively on organization rules for student instruction, for example, James Anderson's study of Baltimore teachers neglects critical differences in the nature of teacher tasks—discipline, instruction, recordkeeping, counseling, etc. Other studies have emphasized the significance teachers attach to such activities as discipline, maintaining order, and dealing with parents. Martin Deutsch claims that as much as 80 percent of classroom time is devoted to discipline-related matters.[34] Haralick found that the manner in which discipline problems are handled is the key determinant of teacher attitudes toward the principal, pupils and parents, and the work situation in general.[35] In sum, the task model attempts to explain teacher behavior in terms of the unique requirements and adaptive mechanisms that characterize different tasks. Teacher attitudes and behavior—indifference to clientele, resistance to innovation, and pathological fear of classroom disorder—are attributed to the inconsistent and ambiguous nature of requirements for performing a wide range of different tasks.

All four models approach the study of schools with a common concern for explaining teacher behavior and attitudes that deviate from the legitimate social aims of schools. Each emphasizes, however, a different approach to explain teacher-client interactions. The social class model stresses the importance of the social background of students both as a determinant of actual school problems and as a criterion by which teachers anticipate problems. It suggests that in schools where students are from predominantly poor families or minority groups, teachers are likely to place preservation of authority and order maintenance ahead of the intellectual aspects of schooling. The bureaucratic approach emphasizes the dysfunctional consequences of enforcing rules for teacher behavior; it is suggested that adherence to rules overshadows the educational objectives of schools. The teacher attributes theme suggests that the way in which teachers deal with everyday classroom situations is a function of such characteristics as race, middle-class values, sex, age, teaching experience, and education. The task model distinguishes between the kinds of functions teachers perform in the classroom.

These themes suggest the complex manner in which numerous factors may influence the teacher-client relationship, and the variety of explanations one may find for similar phenomena. This study attempts to knit together the main concerns of each approach by testing some of their central tenets. First, however, some key terms will be defined and the research design described briefly.

Student Body Characteristics

Advocates of the social class model argue that the basic work problems teachers confront, and the manner in which they anticipate such problems, are linked to the socioeconomic characteristics of students and parents. Social scientists, however, have long debated the true meaning of socioeconomic status and those components of the term that are useful to explain school-clientele relations, educational achievement, and adult life outcomes.

Since the 1966 Coleman Report questioned the capacity of schools to equalize social class differences in cognitive achievement,[36] there has been considerable work on the relationship among socioeconomic status, education, and economic attainment.[37] This study, which used data from Baltimore City schools, focuses on teacher behavior as the key dimension in delivering educational services to clients. Various economic, social, and educational characteristics of students are considered:

1. *Parent Income:* Percentage of parents of students in the school who report yearly income under $4,000.[38] A high-income school is defined as one in which 0% to 26% of the parents report income under $4,000; a low-income school is one in which 27% to 99% of the parents report income under $4,000. The mean for all elementary schools in the study is 26.6%.
2. *Student Race:* A predominantly black school is defined as one in which 0% to 5% of the students are white. A racially mixed or predominantly white school is one in which 6% to 100% of the students are white.[39]

3. *Average School Achievement:* Average grade scores on the Iowa
   Test of Basic Skills of grades three, four, five, and six, were
   weighted by the number of students in each grade, added together, and then divided by the four grades. A low-achievement
   school is defined as one in which the average score is 3.0 to 3.9; a
   high-achievement school is one in which the school average is 4.0
   to 5.4.
4. *Truancy Rates:* Percentages of students in the school absent 40 or
   more days during the 1970-71 school year; such lengthy absence,
   usually due to truancy, often indicates the level of discipline problems within a school. A low truancy school is defined as one where
   the rate is 1% to 9%; a high truancy school is one where the rate is
   10% to 19%. In no school studied was the truancy rate greater
   than 19%.

All four measures of student body characteristics are closely related.
Achievement and truancy rates are educational attributes frequently associated with race and income. In this study achievement, for example, is
strongly associated with race ($Q = .88$), truancy ($Q = .77$), and parent income ($Q = .66$).* In general, these characteristics are a rough measure of
social class climate among the student body, or what is euphemistically
termed "advantaged" and "disadvantaged" schools.

School Bureaucracy

Bureaucracy, according to Max Weber, is technically superior to other
forms of organization.[40] Characterized by a hierarchy of authority, rules
covering rights and duties, and procedures for dealing with work situations, bureaucracy was thought to reduce personal conflict and result in
decisions based upon expertise. In common usage, however, the term
"bureaucracy" more frequently connotes red tape, delay, inertia, inefficiency, arrogance, and rigidity. One objective of this study is to examine
the relationship between structural aspects of bureaucracy in public
schools and those dysfunctional behaviors and attitudes of teachers—such

*Throughout this book, Yule's Q (also called Q) is used as a simple measure of association.
Q is appropriate as a measure of association for qualitative variables arranged in a four-fold
table; it indicates not only the strength of the relationship between the variables, but also
the direction of that relationship. For additional information, see John Mueller and Karl
Schuessler, *Statistical Reasoning in Sociology* (Boston: Houghton Mifflin Co., 1961), pp.
242-249; and Leo Goodman and William Kruskal, "Measures of Association for Cross Clas-
sifications," *Journal of the American Statistical Association,* 1954, vol. 49, pp. 732-764.

as custodial attitudes toward clients, routinization of behavior, and resistance to innovation—with which the term bureaucracy is frequently synonymous.

Public discourse is laced with references to bureaucratic school conditions that stifle creativity, initiative, and responsiveness. The presumption that these conditions are the consequences of bureacracy stimulates suggestions to "debureaucratize" schools through such reforms as vouchers, accountability systems, and community control. By examining the relationship between school organization and some of the alleged teacher consequences of bureaucracy, this study will test, in part, the educational wisdom of such school reorganization.

Previous studies have often assumed that the organizations examined were truly bureaucratic, or that if the school system as a whole were bureaucratic, so must each and every school be likewise. Several attempts to measure bureaucracy empirically indicate, however, that its structural traits exist along a continuum.[41] Some organizations are more bureaucratic than others and some schools are more bureaucratic than other schools.

The basic approach here is to focus on rules and procedures that attempt to regularize, constrain, direct, legitimize, or control teacher behavior in the areas of classroom discipline, instruction, and parent-teacher communication. First, several factors influenced the decision to concentrate on rules for teacher behavior rather than on other criteria of bureaucracy—hierarchy, division of labor, specialization, and so on—because these structural criteria flow from a formal organization chart that varies little between schools, and is rarely determined by each school. Rules of behavior for dealing with specific teaching responsibilities, on the other hand, differ considerably among schools. Second, empirical studies of schools and other organizations find that rules are positively associated with several other bureaucratic dimensions, such as hierarchy of authority, procedural specifications, and impersonality.[42] The relative density of rules may serve, therefore, as an indicator of bureaucracy in general. Third, Robert Merton and others argue that the exercise of hierarchical authority takes the form of rules that specify subordinate behavior.[43] In schools, this means rules about the use of textbooks, curriculum, physical arrangements in the classroom, discipline, punctuality, non-classroom responsibilities of teachers, and so forth. Rules attempt to reduce uncertainty associated with performance requirements for basic tasks, to increase the control of administrators over circumstances in which they cannot be physically present, and to regulate the distribution of authority.

Merton suggests that the emphasis on adherence to formal rules has dysfunctional organizational consequences such as displacement of goals, impersonal treatment of clients, inability to adapt to new circustances, and rigid and ritualistic behavior. Others have identified a "vicious cycle" of escalating rules in which current authority relations are challenged by constitutents, organizational rivals, or subordinates performing key tasks. In an effort to reassert authority, decision-makers promulgate new rules, amendments, modifications, and clarifications. The net result is a system of compulsive rule-making and rule-following, in which the original intent of an organization is obscured by an overriding concern for its rules. Thus, throughout this study, *the measure of school bureaucracy is the level of formal rules for teacher behavior in various classroom tasks.*

Scales of measurement for school bureaucracy commonly exhibit two defects—they ask teachers to draw conclusions rather than to describe the kinds of school rules that actually exist, and secondly, they treat the teaching task as a unitary concept. Examples of the first defect are questionnaire statements such as "I feel that I am my own boss in most matters," "Whatever situation arises, we have procedures to follow in dealing with it," "The teachers are constantly being checked upon for rule violations." These statements demand a highly subjective interpretation by the teacher, and hence provide no benchmark by which to compare the basis of decisions.

The second defect—treating the teaching task as a unitary function—occurs when the researcher focuses on only one aspect of the teaching role, disregarding others that actually may be more important to the teacher. Studies of actual school organization typically concentrate on the instructional task of teachers. Although instruction may be the chief activity related to official goals of teaching and learning, it overlooks those unofficial or informal tasks that may constitute the framework within which daily operating policies and basic decisions of personnel are made. Studies by Becker, Gordon, and Haralick indicate that discipline and the maintenance of classroom order may unnerve a teacher, creating stress and anxiety far greater than problems presented by pedagogical responsibilities.[44]

In order to minimize the shortcoming of totally subjective teacher responses about school organization, this study focused on specific activities of teachers in the classroom. For example, the questions asked dealt with school rules about the preparation of lesson plans, selection of textbooks, children going to the bathroom, meeting with parents. It attempted to deal with the second common defect—treating teaching as a unitary function—by treating school organization of the teaching task as a multidimensional concept. Questions were asked about three aspects of the teaching role: (1) *classroom discipline and order maintenance*, (2) *instruction*, and (3) *parent-teacher communication*. Three separate scales of school organization were developed, one for each area, in order to avoid obscuring intra-school variation between areas of organizational procedure.

Teacher Attitudes

Six teacher attitudes are considered in this essay. They were chosen because of their seeming importance for the quality of the educational service rendered by schools, impact on the teacher-client relationship, and similarity to those cited by Lipsky, James Q. Wilson, Anderson, and Merton. Urban schools are sometimes termed "pathological" in their dealings with clients, largely because attitudes such as these, and the behavior they imply, detract from the legitimate educational and social goals of the school. These attitudes reflect a broad variety of issues ranging from teacher orientations toward important individuals and groups with whom he or she deals, to self-reported information on aspects of classroom management, to the highly volatile issues of parental participation and school innovation in general. (See the Appendix for the specific items used to measure each of the attributes discussed below.)

Custodial Orientation

A teacher's emphasis on disciplinary aspects of the teaching role, extreme sensitivity to the possibility of classroom disorder, and threats to teacher authority indicate a custodial attitude toward students. This attitude or orientation involves a redefinition of the teaching role, in which academic achievement, learning skills, cognitive processes, and student motivation are subordinate to the maintenance of order in the classroom. Where "police" functions of teachers seem to outweigh pedagogical ones, schools may be perceived as dull, authoritarian, custodial institutions.

Classroom Routines

Teachers frequently employ routines in classroom management as a means of increasing everyday efficiency over such common activities as entering and leaving the classroom, going to the bathroom, handing out paper, and getting the class organized. Routines are also intended to establish teacher authority and control over the class. The practice of "grooving the children" is a means of reducing the risk that discipline problems will escalate into more serious disorder. Gordon found that, over a period of years, teachers routinize classroom functions to minimize the personal stress they experience in situations of pervasive conflict.[45]

Attitudes Toward Parents

Most educators agree that parents are vital ingredients in the success of public schools. It has been suggested that hostile teacher attitudes toward parents stem from the nonvoluntary nature of school clientele, difficulty in handling daily classroom responsibilities, and the attempt to externalize blame for educational shortcomings. Others claim that the display of arrogance or indifference toward parents is rooted in a professional ideology that emphasizes teacher autonomy and insulation from public scrutiny. In this study, the scale of teacher attitudes toward parents measures the degree to which parents are *perceived* as disinterested in the school, or fail to appreciate the teacher or inculcate respect for authority, intrude upon areas of teacher autonomy, and have a disruptive influence upon the school.

Parental Involvement

In recent years, the issue of parental participation in school decision-making has become a matter of political contention. Controversies surrounding community control similarly reflect concern with the scope of public participation in school decision-making. Those who favor such changes argue that urban bureaucracies have become unresponsive to the communities they serve. Opponents claim that parents lack the skill, training, and knowledge necessary to make decisions about school personnel and programs.

Educational Innovation

It has been suggested that schools are inertia-bound, enveloped in traditional rules and teaching methods, and reluctant to accept new ideas better suited to the needs of lower-class, nonwhite students. Some have argued that teachers, and teacher organizations, are often allied with opponents of new educational initiatives. Even where school officials seek reform, their attempts may be undermined by the reluctance of teachers to accept these changes. The receptivity of teachers to innovation is but one of numerous factors influencing the capacity of school systems to effect change. Others include the quality of research and development underlying innovations, availability of resources, leadership, public opinion, preparation of staff for change, and the goals and procedures intrinsic to the innovation itself. The more limited aim of of this study, however, is to examine hypotheses regarding the effects of school bureaucracy and school clientele on the acceptance of change by teachers. The study measures the receptivity of teachers to school innovation in general, rather than to any specific proposal. It does so by inquiring about attitudes toward a range of possible innovations, including ones involving new instructional methods, personnel practices, and institutional reorganization.

The Principal

The principal represents the basic source of organizational authority in each school—with major responsibility to specify and direct behavior, arbitrate disputes, clarify roles, and assure a flow of educational resources to teachers in the classroom. The manner in which teachers perceive the principal is an important determinant of their attitudes toward the work situation in general, school clients, and willingness to accept organizational direction. Anderson argues that the principal's exercise of formal authority through the promulgation of rules fosters conflict between bureaucratic and professional sources of teacher role expectations.[46] On the other hand, Robinson found that teachers frequently desire more rules and specific procedures over the work situation than principals are willing to provide.[47] This study seeks to measure the relationship between administrative rules for teacher behavior and the extent to which teachers perceive the principal as backing them up, considering their needs, having their respect, and accepting new ideas and suggestions.

Research Design*

The purpose of this study was to test some of the prevailing themes bearing on the distribution of teacher attitudes toward pupils, parents, the school principal, parental participation in school decision-making, educational innovation, and the use of classroom routines. Its findings suggest policy implications for those interested in issues of school reform. Most of the data in this study were drawn from teacher responses to a written survey questionnaire administered to a sample of Baltimore City

*Those interested in a more detailed explanation of the research methods should read the Appendix.

elementary school teachers during the 1971-1972 school year. Other data come from school principals, records of the Baltimore City Department of Education, interviews, and observation of teachers and other school officials.

At the time the survey was made, Baltimore had just under 4,000 elementary school teachers, of whom 65% were black. They taught 102,000 students, 70% of whom were black. Like that of most other urban systems, the student body of Baltimore schools has become increasingly black: from 1965 to 1971, the proportion of nonwhite students in Baltimore's elementary schools increased 6%, although total enrollment declined. Patterns of *de facto* school segregation were also becoming more severe. From 1960 to 1970 the proportion of segregated elementary schools (defined as schools in which at least 90% of the students are black) grew from 44% to 58%, similar to trends observed in other large urban school systems.

In many other respects Baltimore schools are similar to those in other large cities. At the time the data were collected, Baltimore's declining student enrollment was consistent with the experience in 18 of the nation's 20 most populous cities. Baltimore schools employed over 11,000 people—more than such cities as Boston, Cleveland, Dallas, and San Francisco, but fewer than Chicago, Detroit, and Los Angeles. Baltimore's pupil/teacher ratio (24.3 to 1) was somewhat higher than most large cities, but lower than the ratio of at least five of the largest cities. Per pupil expenditures in Baltimore were approximately $900 a year, a figure higher than such cities as Dallas, Memphis, New Orleans, and St. Louis, but lower than New York, Philadelphia, Washington, D.C., and Cleveland. Similarly, average teacher salaries in Baltimore were higher than at least nine other major cities, but lower than nine other cities. In sum, although Baltimore schools are certainly not a microcosm of all urban schools, neither are they exceptionally different. The Baltimore school system, its teachers and students, share enough characteristics with their counterparts in other large urban schools to make these findings relevant to schools in other cities.

Selecting the Sample

In selecting a sample of teachers, all elementary schools in Baltimore were cross-stratified on the basis of size of the student body and the percentage of parents with income under $4,000. Presumably, this assured some variability on the key dimensions of *school organization* and *clientele characteristics*. Schools with small enrollment have fewer teachers, and probably very different patterns of administration, than those with many teachers. The percentage of parents with incomes under $4,000 is an important, although imperfect, measure of the socioeconomic status of students. A low SES school is one with a high proportion of parent incomes under $4,000; a high SES school, one with a low proportion.

Schools serving only special clientele, such as mentally retarded or physically handicapped students, were excluded. In addition, very small schools, such as those with only one or two grade levels, were eliminated from the sample. This left 145 elementary schools in the total population, from which 31 schools were randomly selected in the final sample.

General classroom teachers from the third, fourth, fifth, and sixth grades were asked to participate in the study. Two hundred twenty usable questionnaires were returned; the response rate was 70%. The need to assure anonymity to teachers prevented a follow-up study to identify bias among teachers who failed to return a questionnaire. The pattern of returned questionnaires was fairly even, however, suggesting no apparent bias in the kinds of schools from which teacher responses were obtained. In addition, comparing known characteristics of all teachers in the 31 schools sampled with those who actually participated in the study reveals no major discrepancies on such potentially significant factors as sex, age, race, experience, and tenure status.

Measurement

Two questionnaires were used in this study. The Principal Questionnaire simply elicited information on race, age, sex, teaching experience, education, and experience as a principal. The Teacher Questionnaire dealt with three subjects—the social and professional characteristics of the teacher, school rules that apply to teacher behavior, and teacher attitudes. Several months were spent interviewing and observing teachers in the classroom, in order to obtain information about specific behavioral and attitudinal items that have meaning for, and distinguish among, teachers. An initial questionnaire was written, pretested on a sample of teachers, and revised.

From responses to the final questionnaire, Guttman scales* were developed to measure the basic dimensions of bureaucratization of teacher tasks and such teacher attitudes as hostility toward pupils, resistance to parental participation in school decision-making, resistance to innovation, routinization of classroom behavior, and hostility toward the principal.

Summary

The preceding discussion describes the major role that teachers play in the political process, and suggests that teacher behavior and attitudes are important determinants of the way in which citizens perceive the delivery of educational services, and to some extent, the way in which school resources are truly allocated. Arguments for changes in current practices related to school organization, decision-making processes, teacher training, and recruitment and promotion policies, rest strongly, although not exclusively, on premises related to the nature of daily interaction between teachers and clients.

There are, of course, other perspectives from which to view teachers within the political system. Schools serve as socializing agents, and teachers may have a significant role to play in the early formation of childrens' political attitudes and values. In addition, to the extent that teachers may influence the acquisition of basic skills, knowledge, and analytic abilities, they may also shape the subsequent life chances of their students as adults. Nevertheless, in the daily interaction between the teacher and client, a significant dimension of the political system goes unobserved by normal political analysis. In the following chapters, we examine the way in which teacher attitudes toward major aspects of daily performance are shaped by the nature of school clientele, bureaucratic school organization, and the individual attributes of the teachers themselves.

---

*The Guttman scale, also known as scalogram analysis, is a method of measuring attitudes (or other attributes) so that the items are ordered, cumulative, and unidimensional. Items are arranged so that an individual who responds positively to any particular item also responds positively to items having a lower rank. If the items can be so arranged, they are said to be scalable. The coefficient of reproducibility is calculated to determine whether items are scalable and unidimensional. For additional discussion of Guttman scales, see the Appendix of this book and Allan Edwards, *Techniques of Attitude Scale Construction* (New York: Appleton-Century-Crofts, 1957), pp. 172-198; Abraham N. Oppenheim, *Questionnaire Design and Attitude Measurement* (New York: Basic Books, 1966), pp. 143-151; Samuel Stouffer et al., *Measurement and Prediction* (New York: John Wiley & Sons, 1950); and Warren Torgerson, *Theory and Methods of Scaling* (New York: John Wiley & Sons, 1967), pp. 307-336.

II

Traits of Students and the Nature of School Personnel

One of the dominant concerns of any political system is the manner in which government policies, programs, decisions, and practices distribute benefits to groups and individuals. Government hiring practices, contracts and grants, administrative decisions, and service delivery often appear to favor middle- and upper-class interests over those of the poor or working-class. Both among and within school districts, it has been alleged that middle- and upper-class areas are favored in the distribution of tangible material resources and school personnel over lower-class areas. Generally speaking, both defenders and critics of urban schools seem to agree, at least superficially, that the inner-city school needs more of whatever constitutes "good education" in the suburban setting—modern buildings, new books, better teachers, closer rapport between professionals and parents, and so on. These inequalities are frequently expressed as differences in student achievement, dissatisfaction with schools, and school-community conflict.

Although it is widely agreed, by both defenders and critics of urban schools, that the classroom teacher is hindered by antiquated school buildings and inadequate remedial services and other resources, explanations for these deficiencies are likely to be quite different. The

defenders—often professional groups, teachers, unions, and supervisors—are likely to blame inadequacies on a lack of community
support—rejected school bonds, low budgets, and political interference
with schools. Outspoken school critics, such as advocates of community
control, are more likely to attribute differences between rich and poor
schools to the pervasive pattern of inequality characteristic of society's
institutions generally. They argue that school officials lack the social and
personal attributes to use material resources effectively in the communities where they work, and thus should be subject to the control of
community residents.

In chapter one it was noted that the race and economic status of
clients often appear to determine inequalities among schools and the
nature of relationships between teachers and pupils. In this study, income
and race of clients strongly correspond to some significant educational
differences among schools. With few exceptions, in this sample the
schools in which parent income is low have the highest truancy rates and
lowest student achievement. Similarly, 81% of the students in predominantly black schools are also in schools with lowest student achievement, whereas 78% of the schools with a larger white enrollment are also
schools with high student achievement.

The notion of unequal material school resources offers an appealing
though illusory explanation for the education gap between students from
rich and poor, white and black areas of the city. In the sample of schools
studied, observation of physical plants and material resources available
revealed no apparent bias in favor of schools in middle-class or white
neighborhoods. Schools in the poorest neighborhoods were as likely to be
modern, or dilapidated, as were schools in more affluent areas. If anything, largely as a result of federal funds, some inner-city schools had
special programs that afforded them an abundance of tangible resources
and facilities relative to other schools in the city system. In addition, the
Coleman Report[1] found that: (a) although minorities were at a disadvan-
tage in terms of tangible school resources, majority-minority differences
were more a regional than a national phenomenon; (b) inequitably distri-
buted material resources have only a minor effect on student performance; (c) differences among teachers have a stronger (although still
modest) correlation with variations in student achievement, particularly
for poor and black students; and (d) home, rather than school, factors are
the most important determinants of educational achievement.

Although distinctions between good and bad, effective and ineffective, teachers typically rest more on personal testimony than on empirical
measurement, many of the contentious issues in school politics focus upon

attributes of teachers in favored and disfavored neighborhoods. Certain characteristics of teachers are conventionally considered educational assets by a community, whereas others may be liabilities. For example, it is asserted that teachers with the least competence, experience, and professional qualifications are clustered in inner-city schools, whereas more affluent schools have the best trained and most competent teachers. For lack of better indicators, credentials, tenure status, educational training, and years of experience are frequently considered surrogates for expertise and teaching competence. In addition, some have asserted the need for more black and male teachers, particularly in inner-city schools, to serve as role models for students.

Beyond demographic composition of school faculty, the general atmosphere of inner-city and suburban schools is said to differ; teachers are said to differ on key attitudes—their learning expectations for students, their emphasis on custodial control and their readiness to innovate, and so on. Inner-city schools are pictured as authoritarian, rigid, custodial-minded institutions; schools in more affluent neighborhoods are perceived as somewhat more flexible, innovative, and learner-oriented. Although these distinctions are gross, they rest upon some assumptions about the attitudes and behavior of teachers. Inner-city teachers are said to have low expectations for students, to emphasize the control functions of the school, to perceive parents as threats to teacher authority and to resist their participation in school decision-making, and to oppose other innovations representing changes in educational and organizational practice. This chapter explores several aspects of this client-teacher relationship.*

Dimensions of the Social Class Model

The *social class model* reflects a general belief that low SES schools do not receive a fair share of the most desired educational resources, including capable teachers. Beyond apparent differences in educational achievement of students, several alternate themes consistently arise concerning the distribution of teachers within the urban school system. Educational disparities have been discussed in terms of culture gaps, patterns of horizontal teacher mobility to middle-class neighborhoods, and the superior professional qualifications possessed by teachers in the "better" schools.

---

*As discussed in chapter one, for purposes of simplification the terms "low SES" and "high SES" are used when referring to characteristics of the student body in general.

The *culture gap argument* implies that teachers, middle-class in origin and values, are unable to appreciate or deal with the particular educational problems of poor, mostly black, students. Its adherents maintain that social attributes of teachers—race, sex, and upbringing—do not provide them with skills and sensitivities essential to the needs of inner-city children. Among the issues raised are (a) whether white, middle-class teachers bring racial and class prejudices to the school that affect their performance, (b) whether inner-city students need black and male teachers to serve as authority figures, to bolster self-esteem, and to facilitate the learning process, and (c) whether the racial and economic background of teachers is so different from that of their students that it gives rise to insurmountable communication barriers, hostility, and misunderstanding.

The *horizontal mobility* thesis suggests that experienced teachers tend to transfer from inner-city to middle-class schools at the earliest opportunity. Howard Becker has noted that school transfer policies often allow teachers to seek new positions after several years; from the perspective of basic problems they confront, teachers often consider these new opportunities because they offer easier and more rewarding places in which to work.[2] The ghetto school is thought to end up as the training ground for inexperienced teachers, many of whom will either prove inadequate or eventually practice their refined skills in middle-class suburban settings.

The *professional credentials* argument is a by-product of the previous one. It suggests that the most competent teachers are found in middle-class schools, largely as a result of the transfer process. A high proportion of teachers in inner-city schools are substitutes, recent college graduates, and otherwise deficient when judged by the conventional criteria, such as training, certification status, and experience. Ghetto schools are thus said to be left with large numbers of teachers who have yet to prove their ability, who may find they dislike teaching, or who, because of minimal skills and credentials, are unattractive to schools in middle-class areas.

Patterns of Teacher Distribution

The following section examines differences in the attributes of teachers among schools serving lower-class students, and those with largely middle-class and upper-class enrollments. Attention is paid to those characteristics—race, sex, education, experience, and certification status—that might support or disconfirm any of the four propositions just cited.

Race

Schools serving the least advantaged students—those who are poor, black, have low achievement and high truancy rates—were found much more likely to have predominantly black faculties than were schools serving middle-class, white students. Of the 31 schools sampled, only two with more than 65% black enrollment have majority white teaching staffs. The picture that emerges is one of strong congruency between the race of students and the race of teachers.

This pattern is similar to the school system as a whole, where approximately 70% of the elementary school students are black, and 65% of the teachers are black. Furthermore, in elementary schools of 90% or more nonwhite enrollment, 86% of the faculty are also nonwhite.[3] This suggests that the great majority of black students are being taught by black teachers, particularly in the inner-city schools.

Social Class Origins

A major tenet of the culture gap thesis is that school systems hire predominantly middle-class teachers and thus educational practices come to reflect the biases of that social background. It has been noted that such teachers may see a kind of "moral unacceptability" in the action or appearance of slum children. Educational failure, hostility, or apathy of lower-class students may thus be attributed to a clash with cultural values held by middle-class teachers. When the social backgrounds of teachers in low and high SES schools was compared, the occupation of father (or head of family) was grouped into two categories indicating relatively low and high occupational status. Some major findings stand out:

—Most teachers in the sample (71%, $n = 218$) were from lower- or working-class origins. As adolescents, their family head was either frequently unemployed, on welfare, or employed in an unskilled, blue-collar, semi-skilled, or clerical position.
—In schools on the low end of the SES scale (low student achievement, predominantly black, high truancy), teachers were more likely to have come from low social status backgrounds themselves (approximately 77%) than were teachers in schools with more advantaged students (63%).

Examination of the race and social origins of teachers sampled indicates a strong correlation between their social attributes and those of their students. Faculties in lower-class, predominantly black schools consist of teachers with racial and socioeconomic backgrounds similar to those of their students. Several explanations are plausible—a policy of allocating teachers to certain schools on the basis of race or class origin, or perhaps the natural attractiveness of particular schools for teachers with racial and social class attributes similar to those of most students in the school. In any case, there is little evidence to support the culture gap notion that students from poor, black families have teachers from "better" backgrounds.

Some have suggested that current social status and future aspirations of teachers, most often middle-class and upwardly mobile, are more important determinants of relations with clients than is their socioeconomic origin. It is argued that, after having escaped lower-class status, teachers may vigorously reject all that characterizes lower- and working-class life styles, much of which reminds the teacher of his or her own origins. The culture gap, therefore, may be most prominent among teachers for whom the role of teacher represents economic and social mobility, and for whom everyday association with lower-class clients is an unpleasant reminder of their own family background.

The effects of socioeconomic mobility of teachers on their relations with students are inconclusive. Among teachers in low income schools, those from middle-class origins are somewhat more likely to express custodial attitudes (64%) than are teachers who grew up in lower- and working-class families (52%). Teachers whose lower-class origins are similar to those of their clients are slightly more inclined to regard their students sympathetically than are teachers who have never really experienced the poverty their students have. This finding suggests that the attainment of middle-class status is not, as some have suggested, accompanied by attempts from teachers to disassociate themselves from their past. Instead, some teachers who were born and raised in middle-class surroundings, never having experienced ghetto life, may be seriously unprepared to cope with the cultural barriers between themselves and their inner-city students. For most teachers, however, social-class origins have little impact on subsequent attitudes toward students.

Sex

During the mid-1960s, the Moynihan Report documented a pattern of matriarchal households among inner-city residents.[4] Since then, many of the discipline and educational problems of ghetto schools have been attributed to the lack of appropriate male role models and authority figures. Although the great majority of teachers sampled were female, lower-class schools have a slightly higher proportion of male teachers than do schools serving middle- and upper-class students; males constitute 21% of the faculty in low-achievement schools, but only 10% in schools with higher student achievement. These findings are similar to those in Herriott and St. John's study of urban school teachers.[5] Although the absolute number of male teachers in lower-class schools may remain insufficient, their distribution within the school system suggests some attempts to place male teachers in schools where the need is deemed greatest.

Teaching Experience

Many have argued that a pattern of horizontal mobility from lower- to middle- and upper-class schools characterizes the careers of urban school teachers. One consequence is to deprive inner-city students of teachers who are presumed to be the most competent, skilled, and experienced. Herriott and St. John confirm this general pattern.[6]

TABLE 1. STUDENT BODY CHARACTERISTICS AND
TOTAL TEACHING EXPERIENCE AMONG FACULTY

Student Body Characteristics	Teachers with Four or More Years Experience (N = 558)	
	%	n
Achievement		
Low	65	252
High	62	306
Percent White		
Low	71	263 *
High	56	295
Truancy		
High	71	246 *
Low	58	312
Parent Income		
Low	67	248
High	60	310

*$p \leq .10$ (Based on confidence intervals for Yule's Q; for the method used in computing these, see James A. Davis, *Elementary Survey Analysis* [Englewood Cliffs: Prentice-Hall, 1971], pp. 57-58.)

Source: Data on teaching experience obtained from Baltimore City Department of Education, Division of Research, "Elementary School Staffing Patterns and Class Size Study, 1971-1972."

Table 1 presents the distribution of experienced teachers among schools in lower-class and more affluent settings. The findings do not indicate a pattern of horizontal teacher mobility. Teachers in predominantly black, high truancy schools are more likely to have at least four years teaching experience than are their peers in largely white or low truancy schools. Measures of student achievement and parent income are negligibly related to the level of teaching experience among the faculty.

We also examined the number of years a teacher has spent in his or her current school. Teachers in low and high SES schools differ slightly in the length of teaching experience in their present schools. A majority of teachers sampled in the lower SES schools have four or more years experience in their present school; in schools with middle- and upper-class students, teachers are likely to have less than four years experience in their current school. A key finding is that among teachers in predominantly black schools, 61% have four or more years experience; the corresponding figure in schools with larger white enrollment is only 48% ($p \leq .10$).

Teachers in Baltimore's ghetto schools have more job experience than their counterparts elsewhere in the city. No doubt some teachers do transfer from inner-city to less difficult teaching situations; however, the general pattern that emerges is one in which blacks, males, and teachers from lower- and working-class origins are concentrated in the lower-class, predominantly black schools. Once there, these and other teachers tend to remain in their schools longer than do teachers in more affluent, white schools. So far, in this study, there is little that confirms the stereotype that inferior or undesirable teachers are disproportionately clustered in schools serving lower-class clients.

Education and Tenure

Two additional indicators of faculty "quality" are educational levels and tenure status. School systems encourage teachers to update their professional training by taking graduate-level courses and obtaining advanced degrees. Teachers are offered higher pay for master's and doctoral degrees obtained. Such degrees presumably constitute superior teaching credentials; thus, advanced degrees may be one indirect measure of the level of professional competence among the faculty. There does not appear to be any difference in the level of professional training (percent with master's degree) among teachers of inner-city students and those in more affluent, largely white, high achievement, low truancy schools. A relatively low proportion (10% to 15%) of teachers in all schools sampled have obtained advanced degrees.

Another indirect measure of professional competence is "election" to tenure. After two years of probation, a teacher possessing the necessary educational requirements and a satisfactory rating by supervisors may be selected for tenure. In addition to providing job security, this is supposed to signify that, after a period of on-the-job training, the teacher had been judged competent by some general professional criteria.

Many critics point to abuses within the tenure system, but in the absence of any direct performance measures, many others consider tenure, along with experience and education, to be crude criteria of competence, and ones with considerable meaning for the allocation of school system resources. Schools with few tenured teachers may be judged to lack the kind of teacher quality implied by "election" to tenure. Undoubtedly, many probationary and substitute teachers will eventually acquire tenure, but the primary recognition of their professional competence has not yet been granted. This study found virtually no difference between low and high SES schools in the proportion of tenured faculty. In any particular school, approximately 60% to 70% of the teachers have achieved tenure. Coupled with findings that inner-city teachers are among the most experienced in the school system, the data do not suggest a systematic pattern of teacher mobility or that ghetto schools are simply training grounds for teachers who will soon seek jobs elsewhere.

Summary

Findings about the Baltimore schools sampled in this study diverge at several points from the results of previous studies. Herriott and St. John found the least experienced teachers in low SES schools.[7] In this study, income of parents is negligibly related to total teaching experience of faculty members, or to experience in their present school. However, teachers in predominantly black schools were found to have a higher level of total experience in their current schools than teachers in largely white schools.

This study found little difference between low and high SES schools in the proportion of their faculty members holding master's degrees, as did Herriott and St. John. Neither did it find a higher percentage of tenured faculty in middle-class or white schools, which suggests that professional credentials of faculty members are not necessarily superior in middle-class neighborhoods. Both studies indicate that male teachers, blacks, and those from low social status origins are clustered in schools serving students from similar racial and economic backgrounds.

Low SES schools are in a favored position in terms of the distribution of several social and professional attributes of teachers that may be considered assets—race, sex, and experience of faculty. They are not disadvantaged in terms of other assets such as advanced degrees, or tenure among faculty. From this perspective, there is little data to confirm various theories of inequity—based upon culture gaps, horizontal mobility, or inferior professional credentials—among the teachers sampled.

There are several plausible explanations for this distribution of teacher characteristics. Perhaps the most benign view is that experienced and well-trained teachers opt to work in ghetto schools as a more stimulating and challenging environment. Another explanation is that Baltimore City policy and administrative practice deliberately restrict the movement of teachers out of the inner city. Although the study revealed no official school policy calculated to increase the proportion of black, male, and experienced teachers in poor areas, administrative practices occasionally encouraged this result. Several teachers in the study had been transferred, on the initiative of supervisors, back into inner-city schools. None of the teachers interviewed suggested any punitive motives for these transfers. Undoubtedly, school officials are sensitive to charges of shortchanging low SES schools; they may use administrative discretion to ensure that the proportion of male, black, experienced, and well-trained teachers in low SES schools compares favorably with that in middle-class schools.

A third explanation for the findings deals with the geopolitical relationship of Baltimore City to the surrounding county school system. As the Baltimore City school system becomes increasingly black and poor, white teachers are attracted to the surrounding, predominantly white, county schools. White teachers purchase homes in the county and seek positions nearby; black teachers, on the other hand, perhaps as a result of suburban residential discrimination, are less likely to live in the county, and consequently, to seek positions in the county school system. With fewer largely white or middle-class city schools in which to work, many of the highly experienced white teachers (often living in suburbs) transfer from city to county schools, or never teach in the city at all. Black teachers, on the other hand, have less incentive or opportunity to transfer, thereby allowing city schools with predominantly poor, black enrollment to accumulate the most experienced teachers.

The findings in this chapter are inconsistent with much conventional wisdom; students in ghetto elementary schools are taught by some of the most experienced and well-trained teachers in the school system. In addition, where students are black and poor, so too are most teachers likely to be black and originally from lower-class families. Although these findings do not support the social class model of gross differences in the quality of teachers among rich and poor schools, neither do they completely disconfirm the argument. The best teachers may leave city schools for teaching positions in the county, but we can only speculate about this possibility. More important, perhaps, is that the measures of race, education, certification status, and teaching experience commonly used may be too gross to reveal subtle distinctions between rich and poor, black and white schools. The distribution of educational resources in schools of different SES may also be measured in terms of teacher attitudes—toward job, students, parents, principal, and issues of educational policy. The second part of this chapter examines the attitudinal differences between teachers in schools of low and high SES.

Student Body Characteristics and Teacher Attitudes

A study by Eric Hanushek suggested that teachers make a difference in student achievement, but those credentials school systems purchase by means of salary incentives do not seem to be important factors.[8] The first part of this chapter examined the distribution of teacher assets that school systems purchase—experience, educational degrees, and tenure. We found a pattern contrary to some prevalent theories: in this sample of Baltimore teachers, the distribution of such tangible teacher assets indicated parity or advantage to the schools with students from predominantly underprivileged backgrounds.

In criticizing the method of measuring school inputs in the Coleman Report, Samuel Bowles has written, "the intelligent formulation of educational policies requires not only a more adequate theory of the learning process under various school and community conditions, but a far more complete description of the school, including such aspects as the atmosphere of the classroom, and more exhaustive measurement of teacher attitudes."[9]

The attitudes of teachers are key determinants of classroom atmosphere and provide an alternative way of examining the allocation of school resources. The issue of equal educational opportunity, however defined, is closely linked to the role played by teachers in the transformation of school inputs into educational outcomes. Factors such as race and economic status of clients are often cited as determinants of the treatment rendered by urban bureaucrats. A typical feeling is that lower-class clients, lacking political power, connections, and other "know-how," may be abused or neglected when seeking to extract benefits from public officials.

Studies of urban bureaucracy contain a similar theme—low-level municipal employees who provide services to the poor or black communities are often charged with insensitivity, unresponsiveness, or middle-class bias against their clients. The same sort of argument has been applied to the urban school teacher. Numerous authors attribute the failure, hostility and apathy of lower-class students to a clash of middle- and lower-class values, racial bias, or general inability of teachers to communicate with students who are black or poor. Others cite the self-fulfilling nature of lower performance expectations, and custodial behavior based upon a highly personalistic sense of threat on the part of teachers.

Herriott and St. John subjected some of these ideas to empirical verification. They found that teachers in lower-class schools are more likely than those in high SES schools to have low morale, seek a new position, and express dissatisfaction with their students.[10] In addition, they found that teachers in low SES schools are less likely to exhibit general competence, innovativeness, or an interest in the students. In his study of junior high school teachers in Baltimore, James Anderson found a quite different pattern. Teachers in lower-class schools are generally less resistant to innovation and less inclined toward impersonal treatment of students than are teachers of middle- and upper-class pupils.[11] Peter Rossi has made similar observations.[12] In short, the evidence is not conclusive that teachers in inner-city schools are likely to have less desirable attitudes toward their roles and responsibilities than do teachers in more affluent settings.

The remainder of this chapter examines the relationship between student characteristics and teacher attitudes toward students, parents, and issues germane to the organizational vitality of public schools. The focus is on custodial attitudes of teachers, routinization of student behavior, hostility toward parents, parental participation in school decision-making, and teacher attitudes toward innovation in general.

Custodial Orientation

Inner-city schools have been described as custodial institutions, more attuned to controlling students and preventing disorder than to teaching and learning. Teachers in such schools, it is said, subordinate pedagogical tasks to discipline and order maintenance. According to Spady, the custodial function of schools is largely a product of compulsory school-attendance laws;[13] these laws compel students to attend school through mid-adolescence, and concomitantly, force schools to accept students who would otherwise choose to be elsewhere. As a result, the school serves clients whose participation is often involuntary.

Teachers sometimes protest that inner-city schools are very difficult places in which to work, because they present serious problems not existing in other schools. Teaching methods must recognize the need to maintain order in the classroom. This study does not dispute this argument, but focuses on that end of a relative custodial-orientation scale in which students are consistently perceived as disrespectful, in need of strict control, and threatening to teacher and school authority. Teachers of such students may develop custodial attitudes in order to maintain their personal and professional dignity. They may emphasize the need for superior-subordinate relations, minimal risk-taking, and special efforts to maximize teacher authority.

Among the teachers sampled, the distribution of custodial attitudes is in the predicted direction—teachers in low SES schools are more likely than those in higher SES schools to express a strong custodial orientation toward pupils (see Table 2). In the lower SES schools— particularly those

TABLE 2. STUDENT BODY CHARACTERISTICS AND
CUSTODIAL TEACHER ATTITUDES

Student Body Characteristics	Teachers Expressing Custodial Attitudes Toward Pupils (N = 220)	
	%	n
Achievement		
Low	54	110
High	40	110 *
Percent White		
Low	51	105
High	42	115
Truancy		
High	52	141
Low	38	79 *
Parent Income		
Low	55	123
High	36	97 ***

*$p \leq .10$
***$p \leq .01$

in which student achievement and family income are low and truancy is high—teachers are more sensitive than their counterparts in upper SES schools to the need for discipline and classroom control.

These findings may be explained, in part, as a response to the stressful nature of the school environment: frequent discipline problems and high rates of absenteeism and transiency are among the circumstances that frustrate performance of the teaching role in lower-class areas. In such schools, teachers experience conflicting role expectations, in which the need to maintain discipline and order competes with an emphasis on instruction, teaching, and learning.

The inner-city teacher may respond to job stress by leaving the profession or transferring to an "easier" school. It was previously observed, however, that relatively few teachers in the study sought transfers: a majority of the teachers in inner-city schools had taught at least four years in their current school. Another possible response to job stress may involve adjustments within the existing situation. Teachers may learn new disciplinary methods and reorient attitudes toward the proper balance between discipline and instructional tasks.

A custodial orientation is a form of role redefinition that orders priorities among competing demands, thereby making the job easier and reducing some of the mental and physical strains upon the teacher. It may involve taking cues from colleagues and supervisors, readjusting role definitions, and developing norms that emphasize discipline and maintaining order. Whether desirable or not, such attitudes equip the teacher with an educational philosophy helpful in ordering behavior on a day-to-day, minute-by-minute basis.

An important problem for administrators is to identify teachers within lower-class schools who are prone to express custodial attitudes. One frequent suggestion is that white teachers, harboring racial and cultural biases, may be the primary source of animosity and mistrust of lower-class students. Surprisingly, however, this study found that in schools considered to have predominantly "disadvantaged" students, black teachers are more likely than are white teachers to express custodial attitudes toward pupils. For example, in high truancy schools, 52% of the black teachers expressed custodial attitudes whereas only 26% of the white teachers did. Although 44% of the black teachers in low-income schools scored high on a scale of custodial attitudes, only 28% of the white teachers did. A similar pattern exists in low achievement and predominantly black schools.

From these data, it appears that black teachers are more inclined than whites to treat poor, black students in a custodial manner. Black teachers in this setting may be able to say and do things to students that white teachers could not. Another plausible explanation is that white teachers in particular experience considerable difficulty in black, inner-city schools. Those that remain in these schools are perhaps teachers with the greatest motivation or commitment to teaching in this difficult environment.

Routinization of Student Behavior

Routines are a basic device of teachers to establish control in the classroom. The implementation of classroom procedures over such seemingly minor items as gum chewing or pencil sharpening involves a system of compliance with the directives of the teacher. The process of "grooving the children" creates habits of obedience, and a system of beliefs regarding acceptable behavior. Lipsky notes that street-level bureaucrats resort to routines in order to reduce resource inadequacy, perceptions of threat, and ambiguous role expectations.[14] By structuring classroom activity into limited and predictable patterns, routines reduce the burden of decision-making for teachers and their level of emotional involvement. Table 3 indicates the distribution of teacher attitudes toward the use of routines in classroom management. Surprisingly, teachers are most in-

TABLE 3. STUDENT BODY CHARACTERISTICS AND THE
USE OF CLASSROOM ROUTINES BY TEACHERS

Student Body Characteristics	Teachers Using High Level of Classroom Routines ($N = 220$)	
	%	n
Achievement		
Low	31	110
High	42	110
Percent White		
Low	25	105
High	47	115[***]
Truancy		
High	34	141
Low	38	79
Parent Income		
Low	32	123
High	42	97

[***]$p \leq .01$

clined to use routines in schools with a high proportion of white student enrollment. In addition, the level of student achievement and income of parents is positively correlated with the frequent use of routines. In short, teachers in congenial middle-class settings use more routines than their inner-city counterparts.

Lipsky suggests that, for street-level bureaucrats, the use of routines and custodial attitudes represents a response to feelings of challenged and fragile authority. This study found a positive correlation ($Q = .32$) between the use of classroom routines and custodial attitudes of teachers—there is a tendency for teachers with a strong custodial attitude to seek support for authority by attempting to routinize classroom behavior. A seemingly paradoxical relationship, however, is the prevalence of custodial attitudes among teachers in low SES schools and routinization of student behavior in higher SES schools. Although there is a tendency for teachers with a strong custodial orientation to use routines in classroom management, the interplay between routines and custodial attitudes, mediated by student body characteristics, is considerably more complex.

Although teachers in lower class, predominantly black, schools are, on the whole, somewhat more likely to express custodial attitudes and less likely to use routines than are their counterparts in more affluent settings, the differences are perhaps overshadowed by some of the similarities among teachers in low and high SES schools. Both low and high SES schools have a large block of teachers (between 31% and 47% of those sampled) who are low both on scales of custodial orientation and on scales of routinization of student behavior. For these teachers, regardless of the school clientele, daily activities proceed in the absence of strong custodial attitudes or heavy, perhaps excessive, reliance on routines in the classroom. Such teachers have apparently struck a balanced relationship so that feelings of threat, ambiguity, and conflict are minimal.

The key difference is that in low SES schools a large proportion of teachers (approximately one-third) express custodial attitudes, but the same teachers employ very few routines in classroom management. The pattern is reversed in schools with a high proportion of middle-income and/or white students: in these schools, almost one-fourth of the teachers tend to routinize classroom behavior even though they eschew the custodial view of teaching.

The overall picture that emerges in one in which substantial numbers of teachers are inclined neither to express custodial attitudes nor to employ excessive routines in classroom management. Where low SES and high SES schools differ, however, is that in the latter there is a tendency toward heavy use of routines unaccompanied by custodial attitudes toward pupils; the opposite pattern is predominant among teachers in low SES schools. Although the elementary-school teacher in a suburban setting is likely to establish numerous procedures for everyday classroom management, so long as they "work," he or she is unlikely to view the classroom as a chaotic setting in which teacher authority is threatened. When classroom routines "work," the authority of the teacher is reconfirmed by student behavior. Where routines break down, the authority of the teacher to control the class and manage common activities is questioned.

Routines serve as a means of controlling student behavior and establishing authority. In accomplishing their purpose, routines reduce the feeling of stress and augment the basic classroom resources of the teacher. In low SES schools, frequent discipline problems may simply overwhelm attempts to enforce routines, causing them to be discarded. Perhaps a narrow range of behavioral deviance, such as is normally found in middle-class schools, will allow the development of effective rules and routines; highly deviant behavior, however, must be dealt with as the situation arises. It follows that if routines accomplish their objective of reducing the perception of threat to teacher authority, they may also facilitate the development among some teachers of a less custodial, more positive orientation toward students. Where routines are more difficult to enforce, as in lower SES schools, a large number of teachers substitute a strong custodial attitude. For some teachers in middle-class schools, the ability to enforce classroom routines reduces the sense of threat to their authority, and thereby minimizes the incentive to adopt custodial attitudes.

Sarason has noted that schools, like most complex organizations, are characterized by behavioral and programmatic regularities—the essential processes and outcomes that characterize school life on a day-to-day basis.[15] On a broad level, regularities may consist in some of the essential functions of schooling, such as the requirement to teach math every day; more narrow regularities refer to the routines by which teachers manage classroom life. There is a substantial disparity, however, between the expectations of new teachers after having completed training and the school regularities to which new teachers are expected to adhere from their first months of teaching. Not surprisingly, when new teachers are advised by colleagues and supervisors to set up classroom routines, they frequently mistake the transmission of school regularities for attempts to control and repress students.

There are some inevitable "reality shocks" that confront any one attempting to apply college-level "book learning" to the real world. For teachers first entering the confusing, sometimes chaotic and conflict-laden atmosphere of many inner-city classrooms, the gap between prep-aration and actual practice may be quite large. After having heard in college about open classrooms, team teaching, motivating students, and the like, initial impressions often leave a sense of frustration and disap-pointment. To fill the gap, teachers soon begin to acquire new expecta-tions, values, and knowledge about school operations. These include the responsibility of teachers to manage classrooms and maintain order. One of the ways in which this occurs is through the use of routines. Teachers often begin their careers with little understanding of such basic proce-dures by which schools operate.

Teacher Attitude Toward Parents

Teachers and parents are, in one sense, partners in the education of children. In many ways their roles are complementary: the teacher de-velops and refines those skills and abilities that have been instilled in children as a result of parental upbringing. In this view, teachers both require and solicit the assistance of parents. Because teachers and parents share overlapping responsibilities, however, there is a large possibility for misunderstanding, disagreement, or antagonism. The teacher may see the parent as intruding on professional autonomy or failing to provide the child with a cultural background sufficient to successfully handle the school program. Conversely, parents may view the teacher as incompe-tent, biased, or indifferent to the educational success of the child.

This study measured teacher attitudes toward parents and toward parental participation in school decision-making. Hostility toward parents reflects the extent to which parents are seen as undermining the teacher's authority between pupil and teacher, infringing upon professional pre-rogatives, and failing to support the school. Resistance to parental partici-pation is both a political issue and a pedagogical one, reflecting the degree to which teachers recognize competing sources of expertise and are will-ing to share authority.

Although attitudes toward parents and parental participation seem unaffected by student characteristics such as achievement levels, truancy, and family income, this study found the following:

—A positive association between the proportion of students who are white and their teachers' hostility to parents ($Q = .21$). As the propor-tion of white students increases in a school, so does the likelihood that its teachers will express hostile attitudes toward parents.

—A positive association between the level of white student enrollment and teacher resistance to parental participation in school decision-making ($Q = .33$, $p \leq .05$). Teacher resistance to parental involvement is strongest in largely white schools.

Previous research suggests two basic reasons for these findings: (a) middle-class parents are more likely to participate actively in school affairs than are parents in lower-class neighborhoods, thereby exceeding teacher thresholds of tolerance for parental involvement; and (b) the content of middle-class participation is more likely to challenge bases for teacher authority.

Several studies indicate that the level of parental participation in any political activity is directly proportional to the socioeconomic status of the neighborhood. Studies by Herriott and St. John, and by M. Kent Jennings, show clear social class differences in the nature of parent-school interaction.[16] In their study of urban schools, Herriott and St. John found that, in low SES schools, parents rarely attend school events or initiate discussion with teachers; the level of parental involvement is higher in middle-class schools, and parents are more assertive about their role in the school. Such parents, many of whom are professionals in other fields, possess expertise and social standing comparable to or greater than that of the teacher. In Jennings's analysis of national survey data from 2,000 parent interviews, as socioeconomic status increased (measured by the proportion of high school seniors going to college), so too did the proportion of parents expressing school grievances and taking specific action to ameliorate them.

Not only does the level of parental participation in school affairs differ between lower- and middle-class parents, but so does the substantive nature of the relationship between school and client. Despite differences in terminology, researchers suggest that middle-class parents generally desire "content" oriented teachers and lower-class parents prefer "control" oriented teachers.[17] A content-oriented teacher emphasizes instruction and learning activities; the control-oriented teacher is most concerned with discipline and order. The middle-class parent complains, therefore, about teachers who appear to emphasize control rather than content, and whose teaching methods diverge from parental preference. The underlying basis of teacher authority—expertise over matters of instruction and the learning process—is continually scrutinized and questioned.

The inner-city teacher, on the other hand, is likely to suffer little outside interference—from parents or administrators—so long as the expectations for discipline and order are satisfied. The teacher in this school may enjoy more autonomy and, so long as the semblance of order prevails, not feel his or her professional authority is threatened by parents challenging classroom practices.

Teachers in upper SES schools have a satisfactory working relationship within the confines of the classroom. Students are seen in favorable terms, as evidenced by the low incidence of custodial attitudes toward pupils. Teachers exercise strong control over the class through the use of rules and routines. Pupils perform reasonably well on achievement tests; it may be inferred that they do as well in the classroom. In short, teachers in largely white, upper SES schools have the easier and better teaching positions according to conventional standards.

In such schools, the cost to the teacher posed by parental participation is particularly great. There is an implicit threat that the status quo may be undermined by new school and classroom arrangements in which parental participation is even more pronounced than it is already. Where teachers find the existing arrangements satisfying and congenial, new authority relationships are likely to be resisted. This argument applies to other teacher attitudes, such as toward school innovation in general.

Teacher Resistance to Innovation

Table 4 indicates that student body characteristics, such as achievement, proportion of white students in the school, and parent income, are positively associated with resistance to school innovation among teachers. Opposition to proposed changes in teaching practices, curriculum, other instruction, and organization arrangements, is greater among teachers in middle-class, largely white schools than it is among teachers in low achievement, low income, predominantly black schools. These differences are statistically significant. In relatively underprivileged school settings, teachers may find few sources of satisfaction in the classroom situation. Poor student achievement, discipline problems, difficulty in obtaining the assistance of parents or principal are common complaints. A tendency toward custodial orientation was found to be one characteristic of teacher attitudes; another is the support of proposals for institutional and pedagogical reform that promises to ameliorate urban educational problems. Conversely, in middle-class schools, teachers have the most to lose from parental participation and other innovations that might undermine their authority; as a result, teachers in these settings exhibit the greatest opposition to organizational and pedagogical school change.

TABLE 4. STUDENT BODY CHARACTERISTICS AND
TEACHER ATTITUDES TOWARD INNOVATION

Student Body Characteristics	Teachers Expressing Resistance to School Innovation (N = 220)	
	%	n
Achievement		
Low	54	110
High	68	110**
Percent White		
Low	52	105
High	69	115**
Truancy		
High	58	141
Low	66	79
Parent Income		
Low	54	123
High	69	97**

**$p \leq .05$

There is a strong association between teacher resistance to innovation and resistance to parental participation ($Q = .42$). With the growing awareness that lower-class parents do not participate in school affairs, compared with middle-class parents (despite relatively benign teacher attitudes), considerable attention has focused on increasing parental participation as an innovation that might be a partial solution to the problems inner-city schools confront. In lower SES schools, claims made by proponents of such reforms have strong appeal to teachers, perhaps because there is little that is attractive in their school situation. For teachers in upper SES schools, however, such a change represents a potential threat to satisfactions derived from present school arrangements.

One of the seeming paradoxes in this study is that despite the receptivity of teachers in lower-class schools to parental participation, efforts to increase it are often accompanied by school strife. In many cases, the meaning of the term "parental participation" is obscured by issues of decentralization and community control of schools, which are so often the basis of political conflict. Parental participation, therefore, has different meanings that depend on the setting in which the issue is raised. In the abstract, the term may suggest a cooperative teacher-parent relationship, in which the boundaries of professional expertise and authority are clearly understood and respected. Among many teachers, parental participation implies a mechanism whereby support for school activities will be induced from previously indifferent parents, and participation will be sparked in parent organizations with a tradition of support for school principal and faculty.

On the other hand, when parental participation is linked to community control, it represents a challenge to the educational hegemony of school officials. Questions are raised about the basis of expertise and authority over decisions ranging from hiring and firing of personnel through curriculum. To the extent, therefore, that the issue of parental participation in school affairs is separate from larger issues of overall school organization, it is likely to receive the bipartisan support of both teachers and parents. Where parental participation is a code word for transferring authority for key decisions from professionals to community, however, the opposition of teachers stiffens considerably.

Conclusions

Considerable attention has been directed at policies to equalize educational opportunities for students from different economic and racial backgrounds. One aspect of this effort has been to reduce alleged disparities in the quality of teachers between schools in poor, black neighborhoods, and those in largely middle-class, white neighborhoods. In this study, there is little evidence to support the argument that middle-class, white, high achievement schools are favored in the distribution of teachers whose credentials and social attributes some consider to be teaching assets. There are negligible differences between low- and middle-income schools in the proportion of teachers with post-baccalaureate degrees or tenure status. Nor is there inequality in these areas among schools with students of various racial compositions, rates of student achievement, or truancy. Contrary to widely held beliefs, predominantly black, high truancy schools are favored in the proportion of experienced teachers (those with four or more years total teaching experience) among the faculty. In addition, the largely black schools have a statistically significant advantage in the percentage of teachers with extensive experience in their current school. With respect to variations in other student characteristics (family income, achievement, and truancy rates) the data show a similar, although less prominent, pattern—schools in disadvantaged neighborhoods have a slightly higher proportion of experienced teachers than do schools in more affluent settings.

In recent years, critics of urban schools have begun to emphasize the social attributes of teachers—race, sex, and family background—as important determinants of educational services and conflict in schools. This study found considerable overlap, however, between the social characteristics of students and teachers in the schools sampled. There was a particularly strong congruence between the racial composition of the student body and that of the faculty. In addition, low achievement, low income, high truancy schools have a higher proportion of both black teachers and teachers from low social status backgrounds than do schools with more "advantaged" clients. Low achievement schools also have a higher proportion of male teachers than do schools with high student achievement.

Another way to measure the allocation of educational resources is to examine teacher attitudes toward pupils, parents, and the performance of the teaching role. A key variable structuring teacher attitudes is the racial composition of the student body. The study found that teachers in schools with "high" white enrollment were more likely than those in predominantly black schools to express hostility toward parents, and resistance to parental participation in school decision-making and to educational innovation. In white schools, there was also heavier use of classroom routines than in largely black schools. Other findings indicate a positive association between student body characteristics such as parent income and achievement, and teacher routinization of behavior and resistance to innovation. In sum, contrary to conventional wisdom, teachers in middle-class, largely white schools use more classroom routines, and appear more hostile to parents and resistant to parental participation and other school reforms than do teachers in less affluent settings.

One important exception deals with the pattern of custodial attitudes among teachers. The evidence reported here supports what many have argued—that teachers in schools characterized by low achievement and high truancy among students are significantly more inclined to display custodial attitudes than teachers in "comfortable" middle-class schools. In predominantly black schools, teachers were more likely to view students custodially than were teachers in schools with mixed or largely white enrollment.

Recent attempts to recruit black teachers to inner-city schools are justified, in part, by the argument that white teachers respond less favorably than do black teachers to ghetto conditions. The findings in this study do not support this assertion. Surprisingly, there is a tendency for black teachers in poor, largely black schools to express custodial attitudes more frequently than do their white colleagues.

Taken as a whole, these findings raise doubts about some common stereotypes of school inequality. Efforts to attribute disparities in educational achievement or levels of community dissatisfaction with schools to

differences in the quality of teachers between middle-class schools and
inner-city schools are largely unsupported by this study. In general, it was
found that students and parents in inner-city schools may receive equal or
favored treatment when such benchmarks as experience, education, or
tenure status of faculty members are considered. Nor do measures of
teacher attitudes provide convincing evidence that teachers in lower-class
schools are less desirable than those in middle-class settings. Although
teachers of lower-class black students are more likely to express custodial
attitudes, those in middle-class, white schools are inclined to use extensive routines in the classroom and to resist school innovation and parental
participation.

Quite obviously, there is a need for better measures of teacher attitudes and performance than are presently available. From these findings, however, it would be difficult to establish a persuasive connection
between the quality of teachers in inner-city schools and the kinds of
educational outcomes in these schools. Such schools would clearly benefit
from superior teachers. However, among the teachers in this sample,
those in black, low income, educationally "disadvantaged" schools seem
generally responsive and sympathetic to the needs of their clients.
Perhaps the flight of white teachers from city to outlying suburban schools
has dramatically reversed a historic pattern of teacher inequality between
ghetto and middle-class areas *within* the city boundaries.

These findings, although by no means exhausting the range of variables that might be considered, raise questions about the standards by
which school personnel are commonly compared. All too often studies
focus exclusively on the inner-city school and conclude that there is a
relationship between educational outcomes and deficiencies in school
teachers. It may be suggested that the frequent absence of real comparative research gives rise to unfair bases of judgment.

These findings are limited by the scope of the sample, which was
confined to elementary school teachers in one large urban school system.
It is possible to think of the entire metropolitan area, including adjacent
county schools, as a more fitting population of teachers. A sample chosen
in this manner might have altered considerably the nature of differences
between teachers in predominantly black, inner-city schools and those in
middle-class, white schools. The policy reality with which most urban
educators must deal, however, is not some "metro" nirvana, but rather,
the same urban enclave we have studied. These findings suggest that we
know far less about that enclave, in its current condition, than has been
thought.

III

Sources of School Bureaucracy

Few issues have evoked so much concern from citizens and social critics alike as the impact of bureaucracy on all aspects of modern life—work, family, leisure, and the general pattern of social relations. The term bureaucracy suggests large organizations characterized by stifling conformity, rigid interpretation of rules, impersonality, and ritualistic and uncreative performance. Schools are often described as educational bureaucracies—where the interests of clients are subordinate to those of the organization and in which rules are formulated to enhance efficiency and the attainment of educational objectives but often do just the opposite.

The meaning of "bureaucracy" is often confusing. Summarizing its most frequent usage, noted above, Michel Crozier refers to the "maladapted responses of bureaucratic organizations to the needs which they should satisfy, and the frustrations their members, clients or subjects consequently endure."[1] The more traditional but less common meaning, derived from the work of Max Weber, focuses on the pursuit of specified objectives through an organized collective effort. Bureaucracy suggests a concentration of effort and resources within a system characterized by impersonal rules and separation of functions and responsibilities.[2]

49

The different images of bureaucracy bear directly on educational policy concerns regarding the organization of schools. As alleged by Merton and many others, bureaucracy generates a vicious cycle of rule conformity, impersonality, and resistance to change—the classic dysfunctions of organizational life.[3] Many currently debated school reforms, such as decentralization, vouchers, and accountability systems, would transfer considerable authority from principals and superintendents to lay individuals and groups—often in the spirit of "de-bureaucratizing" schools. Because the consequences of bureaucracy suggested by Merton are largely speculative and anecdotal, proposed remedies for the problems of the school bureaucracy may perhaps be unwise. In this chapter, we will consider how various characteristics of school leadership, faculty, and clients are related to differences in the bureaucratic rules by which schools are administered; in the next chapter, we will examine the "maladaptations" allegedly resulting from the bureaucratic nature of school organization.

Organizational Theory

First, let us locate the broad study of organizations in relationship to this essay. For many years, students of organizational behavior were guided predominantly by the work of Max Weber; it was assumed that the bureaucratic organization has an identifiable objective, and that the purpose of bureaucracy is to organize available resources for the efficient and rational pursuit of objectives.

Subsequent organization theorists are frequently categorized as either classicals or moderns. The former designates those such as Fayol, Taylor, Gulick, and Urwick—pioneers in an approach emphasizing the structural characteristics of organizations, such as hierarchy, span of control, and specialization of functions. Since the mid-1950s, modern theorists have been increasingly concerned with the psychological effects of organization on job attitudes and behavior. Research has focused on the capacity of subgroups, informal groups, and individuals to hold objectives different from those of the organization, and thereby to behave in ways that thwart organizational objectives.

In recent decades, attempts to bridge the gap between classical and modern theorists have emphasized the effects of organizational structure on human behavior, and the creation of alternative incentive systems for the attainment of organizational objectives. The work of Simon, Thompson, Etzioni, March, and others is concerned with the means by which organizations obtain the compliance of their members through regulation of the decision-making process. Students have identified numerous organizational practices intended to influence or regulate the behavior of subordinates. These include professional training, recruitment and promotion practices, personal loyalties, and the selective flow of advice and information.

Etzioni suggests three categories of organizational control techniques: coercive, utilitarian, and identitive power.[4] Coercive power refers to the use of threats or fear to intimidate subordinates. The use of corporal punishment is a form of coercion occasionally employed in schools. As noted by Spady, the threat of force tends to be highly unstable, for it is accepted with fear, and lasts only as long as the consequences of noncompliance are thought to be more damaging than preferred alternatives.[5]

Utilitarian power corresponds to the exchange of rewards—teachers get paid and students receive diplomas (which are tickets to adult economic benefits) in exchange for compliance with school norms. Like coercion, utilitarian benefits may be of limited value in influencing the daily behavior of school members. Teacher pay does not differentiate between excellent and minimally acceptable behavior. The best teacher receives the same economic benefits as do less satisfactory performers. For students, the value of the diploma is not immediate but lies in its effect upon future life chances. This also assumes that students have future orientations and will voluntarily comply with school expectations in exchange for future rewards.

Etzioni's third category, identitive power, refers to the manipulation of symbols to control behavior. The role of the teacher symbolizes pedagogical expertise, and therefore, students will normally comply voluntarily with teacher requests. However, when teachers are advised to "establish authority" in the classroom, it suggests that the symbols of teacher expertise may not always be readily acknowledged by students.

In modern organizations, the most typical form of influence is through authority (a term quite similar to identitive power). In its pure form, authority suggests that individuals voluntarily obey directives without regard to their specific content; legitimate authority is therefore obeyed without the fear of coercion or loss of utilitarian benefits. In schools, teachers often believe that they are the legitimate source of authority in the classroom, and parents should support, but not interfere with, the teachers' work. Similarly, the principal is often said to be the supreme school authority, and his or her orders should be obeyed.

Weber distinguishes among several forms of authority: charismatic authority, deriving from the unique qualities of individual leaders; traditional authority, based on a reverence for established customs and institutions; and bureaucratic authority.[6] According to Weber, Herbert Simon, and others, the modern organization is characterized by extensive reliance on bureaucratic authority as a primary basis of influence over the behavior of subordinates.[7] The term "bureaucratic authority" implies a hierarchical ordering of positions in which role behavior, policies, and bases of decision are transmitted through the formulation of rules. Such rules specify the facts and values that constitute criteria of decision-making. In addition to limiting, directing, and authorizing the behavior of subordinates, formal rules protect workers from supervisory caprice or pressures from constituents seeking special favors.

Bureaucratic Authority in Schools

Review of Past Research

Studies of organizational structure have found a wide range in the extent to which bureaucratic authority governs the daily operations of workers in complex institutions.[8] Research in this area emphasizes five basic factors bearing upon the extensiveness of formal rules: organizational size, leadership succession, the nature of goals and tasks, expertise, and relations with clientele groups.

Weber regarded *size* (in the form of aggregates of wealth and people) as a key source of bureaucracy: "the increasingly bureaucratic organization of all genuine mass parties offers the most striking example of the role of sheer quantity as a leverage for the bureaucratization of a social structure."[9] Udy argues that "the larger the organization, the greater the number of subgroups in it; hence, the greater the overall emphasis on formal and impersonal rules and specificity of roles."[10] Gouldner and Blau assert that size is not an inevitable source of bureaucracy, but that it normally produces social forces that in turn generate bureaucratic patterns of organization.[11]

Empirical studies do not conclusively support the suggested relationship between size and bureaucratic structure. In separate studies, McKay[12] and Anderson[13] found a tendency for larger schools to employ the greatest number of formal rules for teacher behavior. However, other studies by Adams, Hall, and Robinson have failed to confirm a relationship between size and bureaucratic structure.[14] Richard Hall, in his study of 75 organizations, concluded that: "neither complexity nor formalization can be implied from knowledge of organizational size. A social scientist conducting research in a large organization would do well to question the frequent assumption that the organization under study is highly complex and formalized."[15]

Leadership succession is another factor affecting the extensiveness of formal rules for the behavior of low-level workers. When a supervisor is replaced, the new leader is frequently required to substitute previously neglected work rules in place of his predecessor's informal pattern of control. Gouldner wrote:

> It is the emergence of the problems of succession which requires that the successor learn and use bureaucratic methods. The presence of these conditions exerts pressure on the successor to organize bureaucratically. He organizes bureaucratically not only because he wants to or because he values these above other methods, but because he is compelled to by the conditions of succession—if he wishes to maintain his status.[16]

Udy deals with the related theme of *turnover* among organizational members. He hypothesizes, "the higher the turnover rate, the more potentially difficult the process of social interaction, and hence the greater the adaptive emphasis on formal rules and specificity of roles."[17] This notion was supported by Anderson's study, which found that experienced teachers were least subject to formal rules of behavior.[18] However, Punch found a positive correlation between the length of time principal and faculty were together in a school and the prominence of bureaucratic rules.[19]

A third major determinant of rules and procedures is the nature of *organizational tasks*. Udy argues that, as tasks become more technical and complex, a resort to bureaucratic rules is increasingly likely;[20] thus sailing a large yacht might require a more bureaucratic division of labor than does sailing a dinghy. Litwak predicts that, where organizational activities are nonrecurrent or nonuniform, one is likely to find a structure that emphasizes minimal specialization, personal relationships, and few rules or *a priori* limits on behavior.[21]

Popiel's inspection of union structure found that formally stated goals and functions contributed to the development of bureaucratic patterns.[22] However, Hall's comparative study of ten organizations indicated no relationship between the specificity of organizational goals and bureaucratic traits such as formal rules.[23] He noted that sales departments were the least bureaucratic parts of most organizations. This finding was attributed to the high level of "person-oriented" communication in such departments. Anderson found English teachers subject to more rules than teachers of science and industrial arts, suggesting that "rules will vary inversely with the routinizability of the activity in which the organization is engaged and with the specificity of goals."[24]

The nature of *expertise* possessed by members of the organization is a fourth variable said to bear on the extensiveness of rules for teacher behavior. Although Weber equated authority with expertise, various authors suggest that the need for formal rules in the work situation is diminished when workers possess considerable training, experience, and knowledge about their tasks.[25] They argue that rules may be used as a substitute for expertise based on job experience or technical training. Robinson hypothesized that "where a school's personnel (principal and teachers) are highly professional, organizational adaptations of the bureaucratic structure will take place to accommodate the professional's views on the desirability and undesirability of an emphasis on certain bureaucratic characteristics."[26] In the absence of extensive training or internalized professional norms, organization members are more amenable to formal rules as a basis of defining roles appropriate to daily behavior.

Robinson's study found a weak negative correlation between the degree of professional characteristics among school personnel and scores on a scale of bureaucratization.[27] In Anderson's research, teachers with tenure (considered a measure of professional competence) were "subject to significantly fewer instructional rules than other teachers, both probationary and special substitute."[28] However, this relationship was mitigated in part by the finding that, in schools with a lower-class student body, all teachers, regardless of training, tenure, or experience, were subject to the same level of organizational controls.

The fifth factor related to the level of bureaucratic rules is the organization's relationship with *clientele groups*. Organizations frequently seek to avoid control by or dependence upon their immediate clients; where clients are regarded as liabilities in obtaining resources and achieving goals, or as not totally competent to judge the quality of services provided, an organization may seek means to increase its own autonomy. Until recent years, congressional scrutiny of Pentagon budgets was impeded by the successful military claim that in matters of national security, civilians should not substitute their judgment for that of the military. By cultivating new sources of public support, invoking appeals for professional autonomy, or coopting competitive leaders, organizations seek to regulate, protect, and control the flow of vital resources.

Another way in which organizations control the movement of resources to clients is by limiting the range of discretion subordinates have over their own daily behavior. Several studies suggest that the drive for hegemony through the use of bureaucratic control patterns is most prominent among agencies serving lower-class clientele.[29] Anderson found that teachers in lower-class communities were subject to more instructional rules than teachers in more affluent areas.[30] Orion White suggests that bureaucratic rules are one vehicle by which middle-class interests preserve their control over organizations serving lower-class clientele.[31]

This broad review suggests some of the factors often thought to be sources of school bureaucracy. Other factors may also affect the pattern of formal rules for teacher behavior. For example, personal attributes such as sex, race, and age of principal or faculty members may have a bearing upon the extensiveness of rules for different areas of teacher behavior.

School Size and Formal Rules

School size has been measured in two ways—by the number of students and by the number of faculty members. The reason for employing two indicators of school size is that the number of faculty and the number of students enrolled, although related, correspond to distinctive subunits of the overall organization. The form of organizational control is likely to differ from one subunit to another. Organizational rules such as those for instruction are directed explicitly at teacher behavior; rules for discipline and parents, on the other hand, are as often intended to control student and parent behavior as they are to regulate teachers. One might expect, therefore, that the nature of organizational authority varies with the characteristics of the subunit that is the object of influence.

The relationship between both measures of school size and the extensiveness of formal rules for teacher behavior in areas of discipline, instruction and relations with parents was examined. Some of the findings are:

—Schools with small student enrollment (under 760) tend to have extensive rules for discipline and teacher relations with parents. Schools with large student enrollment (over 760) seem to have the least extensive formal rules in these two areas, which often involve close personal contact between teachers, students, and parents. Only 25% of the larger schools closely regulate discipline matters, and only 44% are heavily involved with rules for parent-teacher interaction. The corresponding figures in schools with small student enrollment are 47% and 60%, respectively.

—There is a small, but positive, association between faculty size and the level of instructional rules ($Q = .32$), confirming the results of the Anderson study.[32] As the size of the faculty grows, so too does the likelihood that formal rules for instruction will replace personal forms of supervision.

These findings suggest that the link between organizational size and formal rules depends in part upon the task or the subunit to which the rules apply. In schools with large faculties, extensive rules regulate instructional activities; in smaller schools, there are fewer such rules. On the other hand, as the number of students in the school increases, there is a decline in the incidence of rules directed toward them—for discipline and for parent-teacher relations.

As noted earlier, the nature of the instructional task differs considerably from the job of disciplining students and dealing with parents. The former is aimed exclusively at teacher behavior. In contrast, discipline rules are partly directed at helping the teacher control behavior of deviant students. Similarly, rules for parent-teacher relations (such as those concerning classroom visits) are in large part connected with regulating the parent as well as the teacher.

A second difference concerns the primary source of teacher expertise in each area. Instruction is subject to a wide range of professional norms, in which extensive training and socialization provide a base of knowledge from which to formulate rules and secure adherence from teachers. Reading techniques, learning processes, testing, and evaluation of students are a few of the instruction-related areas emphasized during teacher training and certification tests. Discipline and relations with parents, on the other hand, are highly subjective areas of teacher responsibility. Expertise is less dependent on professional training than it is on social skills and experience. This weak basis of formal knowledge inhibits the implementation of formal rules for two reasons:

—Suitable rules are not readily apparent to administrators. The highly personal, nonrecurrent nature of tasks makes it quite difficult for administrators to anticipate the varied circumstances required for rule formulation.

—Rules are difficult to implement where authority is weakly supported by professional expertise. The absence of professional authority in areas of discipline and relations with parents reduces the legitimacy of rules in the eyes of those who must adhere to them; the basis of authority is particularly precarious where rules are directed at clients who do not share professional norms compatible with those of school officials.

The qualities associated with discipline and parent-teacher relations illustrate the limits on rule-making in large organizations. Rules for discipline and relations with parents are difficult to establish because they derive less from formal authority and expertise than from personal understandings and accommodations. They also require compliance from nonprofessionals—students and parents. Diversity among all the members of a large school makes development of such rules quite difficult. The result is that teachers in large schools often have a wide range of discretion in handling such tasks as discipline and relations with parents.

In contrast, the instructional task is characterized by a positive correlation between faculty size and formal rules. In this area, rules focus exclusively on teacher behavior, generally without the need for securing compliance from nonprofessional sources. In addition, the instructional task itself is subject to considerable predictability, planning, and technological control —through books, lesson plans, and curriculum requirements. As a result, large schools are capable of directing faculty behavior through the use of formal rules for instruction. Small schools may use other methods such as observation between supervisor and teacher.

The writings of many theorists presume a direct association between the size of an organization and reliance upon formal bureaucratic rules to guide the behavior of employees. The present findings suggest, however, that such a relationship depends on the kind of tasks in which the organization is engaged. Where basic activities are complex and diverse, some tasks are more likely than others to be governed by extensive rules. Tasks that are highly subjective, that involve personal judgments in unplanned, nonrecurrent situations, are likely to have fewer rules for teacher behavior as the size of the school increases. On the other hand, tasks that are relatively circumscribed by their technical nature are often subject to a greater degree of bureaucratic control as the size of the organizational unit increases. This does not mean that administrators making the rules are less interested in discipline than instruction. Rather, the distinctly different nature of these tasks makes one area more amenable to hierarchical control than the other.

Student Body Characteristics

Numerous authors hypothesize a connection between the racial, economic, and related educational characteristics of the student body, and the prominence of bureaucratic control mechanisms —bureaucratic rules serving as the vehicle by which middle-class interests regulate the flow of resources and preserve control of lower-class clients. The findings in Table 5 indicate the following:

—Educational attributes typically found in inner-city schools (low achievement and high truancy) are positively correlated with bureaucratic rules for student discipline; these settings are more likely to have extensive rules for student discipline than schools with high achievement and low truancy.
—Schools in middle-class settings (with few truants and few poor familes) tend to have a higher level of rules for parent-teacher relations than do schools with many truants and many low-income families.
—Characteristics of the student body have little bearing on rules for instruction.
—Racial composition of the student body is unrelated to the pattern of organizational control.

TABLE 5. CHARACTERISTICS OF STUDENT BODY AND LEVEL OF
FORMAL RULES FOR THE 31 SCHOOLS SAMPLED

| Student Body Characteristics | Percent of Schools with High Level of Formal Rules for: | | | |
	Discipline	Instruction	Parent-Teacher Relations	Number of Schools
Achievement				
Low	41	47	53	17
High	29	50	50	14
Percent White				
Low	37	44	50	16
High	33	53	53	15
Truancy				
High	40	50	45	20
Low	27	46	63	11
Parent Income				
Low	39	50	33**	18
High	31	46	77**	13

**$p \le .05$

Teachers in schools with low student achievement and high truancy rates report a higher level of school rules in the area of discipline than do

other teachers. In such schools, discipline problems are a common oc-
currence. Administrators respond with rules designed to assist the
teacher in handling this responsibility. Where teachers are not beset with
numerous discipline problems, they are less likely to pressure the principal for rules stating the precise limits of their responsibility and authority.

Rules also help the principal by reducing the burden of constantly
adjudicating disputes sent to his or her office. Schools with high student
achievement and low truancy usually have less severe problems with
student discipline. In such settings, administrators allow teachers considerably more discretion in handling occasional incidents.

Table 5 indicates that schools with truant problems and those in
poverty areas are also schools with the fewest formal rules for parent-
teacher relations. It is in schools with middle-class clientele—where
truancy is ordinarily quite low and parent income is high—that rules
regarding the relationship between teacher and parent are most prominent. In the previous chapter, it was suggested that middle- and upper-
income parents tend to be frequent, articulate, and assertive participants
in school affairs. The findings in this study reflect an organizational response to the high level of parental activity in middle and upper-income
schools, and the anxiety engendered among teachers by their presence.
Rules may serve to protect authority relationships from challenge. Patterns of teacher behavior may be defended in terms of adherence to
school requirements rather than as a personal decision of the teacher.
Hence, as parental activity increases the threat to teacher authority, so
too does the motivation to create rules stabilizing and limiting the relationship.

Clientele characteristics are negligibly related to the extensiveness of
instructional rules in schools. Authority of principals and teachers in the
area of instruction is largely derived from the formal goals of schooling,
reinforced by professional training and the school system hierarchy itself.
The impact of social class and racial characteristics of students on instructional rules is slight and contrasts strongly with the incidences of rules for
discipline and parent-teacher relations, where the client's socioeconomic
characteristics come into play directly.

Interpretation of this finding varies, depending upon one's
philosophical orientation. If educators in ghetto areas have lower learning
expectations for students, as is often alleged, it is not apparent in the way
schools are organized for instruction. Another way of looking at these
findings, however, is that schools do not readily tailor instructional procedures to fit the different needs of students from varying social
backgrounds. Some might argue that the organization of instructional

tasks in lower-class schools represents an inappropriate adoption of professional norms reflecting organizational practices suitable in middle-class schools.

These findings question the conventional wisdom that administrators manipulate bureaucratic rules to restrict access of lower-class clients or the flow of educational services. Although extensive rules for student discipline are most commonly found in lower-class schools, relations with parents are more closely regulated in middle-class settings. In the area of instruction, socioeconomic factors have little bearing on the development of bureaucracy. A persuasive explanation is that bureaucratic rules are an important mechanism whereby public agencies regulate areas of potential conflict. Where schools feel vulnerable, either because students are unruly or because parents carefully, perhaps zealously, scrutinize all aspects of school life, there are strong incentives to define appropriate behavior before conflict gets out of control. From the viewpoint of school personnel, bureaucratic rules protect them from what may appear to be capricious or irrational criticism.

The School Principal and Organizational Rules

The principal is the chief school administrator, with considerable latitude to implement and enforce rules for teacher behavior. Various social and professional characteristics of principals—such as experience, education, race, sex, and age—may affect the extent to which they exercise hierarchical control through formal rules of behavior.

Experience as a Principal

As discussed earlier, leadership succession is thought to be an important determinant of organizational structure. When a principal is replaced, it may initially be quite difficult for the new incumbent to influence subordinate behavior through such personal ties as loyalty, friendship, and informal discussion. Bureaucratic authority, however, is rooted in the position of the principal, and is therefore a relatively stable form of influence regardless of the particular officeholder. If so, leaders new in a school might be more likely to rely on rules and regulations to control subordinates. (See Table 6.)

TABLE 6. LENGTH OF EXPERIENCE AS PRINCIPAL IN
CURRENT SCHOOL AND LEVEL OF FORMAL RULES

| Principal's Experience in Current School | Percent of Schools with High Level of Formal Rules for: | | | |
	Discipline	Instruction	Parent-Teacher Relations	Number of Principals ($N=29$)
Less Than Four Years	40	53	60	15
Four Years or More	28	43	43	14

Those principals who have been in their schools for more than four years rely minimally on formal rules of behavior for teachers; recently assigned principals are more inclined to use extensive rules. This reaffirms the findings in Gouldner's study, in which an administrator with considerable longevity relied on a wide range of informal practices and understandings to get things done.[33] His successor lacked these relationships, and therefore made extensive use of formal rules and directives.

An evolution in the pattern of organizational control takes place over time. Initially, principals use formal rules and directives because they are most easily promulgated, communicated, and implemented through hierarchical channels. As the principal deals with teachers on a daily basis, he or she acquires other tools by which to direct behavior—friendship, favors, loyalty, and fear are some bases of influence. In addition, rules that are in effect a long time may eventually be transformed into a system of beliefs and understandings among teachers, such that the rules themselves are no longer recognized as a basis of behavior.

The longer a principal heads a school, the more likely he or she is to administer with methods other than impersonal rules. In contrast, cumulative experience as a principal in all schools has little bearing on the level of organizational rules for instruction and parent-teacher relations. There is a strong negative association, however, between the length of total experience as a principal and formal discipline rules ($Q = -.70$)—the least experienced principals are the most likely to rely on such rules.

Becker and others note that teachers expect strong support from the principal in the area of discipline.[34] In this study, those principals with recent teaching experience were found most likely to meet this expectation with formal rules for student discipline. Relatively inexperienced principals believe that they will be judged largely on their ability to run an orderly school. Reliance on persuasion and personal familiarity with staff and students may, at first, appear to be an elusive and fragile basis of control.

Education of the Principal

Two criteria commonly used in recruiting school administrators are supervisory experience elsewhere and professional credentials, often postgraduate degrees. We noted above that principals with extensive experience generally avoid heavy reliance on bureaucratic organizational techniques. The effect of advanced academic education on principals' administrative styles is quite different. Principals with M.A.'s, Ph.D.'s, or Ed.D.'s are more likely than those without such degrees to use formal rules for teacher behavior in the areas of discipline and instruction. In the schools studied, 56% of the principals with advanced degrees employed extensive rules for discipline, but only 15% of those without post-baccalaureate degrees did likewise. In the area of rules for instruction, the corresponding figures were 56% and 38%. Educational attainment of principals is of little consequence for the level of rules regarding parent-teacher relations.

These findings suggest that advanced education may provide principals with formal management skills that encourage the use of rules in the areas of discipline and instruction. In contrast, previous findings have indicated that the more experience a principal has, the more he or she tends to use personal skills rather than formal rules to assert authority, particularly in the area of discipline.

Sex, Age, and Race of Principal

The administrative practices of principals may also be related to such personal attributes such as sex, age, and race. Although this study found no significant administrative differences between schools headed by black rather than white principals, it did find that sex and age bear on the organizational style of administrators (the reader should note that with such a very small sample size, any findings should be interpreted with appropriate caution).

Sex. Findings in this study indicate that male principals (42%) are slightly more likely than are female principals (32%) to head schools with many rules for discipline; female principals, however, are more likely to emphasize rules for instruction (58%) and relations with parents (63%) than are their male counterparts (33%). For example, male principals are more likely to stipulate techniques by which teachers can control unruly students and occasions when it is appropriate for teachers to refer discipline problems to the principal or vice-principal. Organizational techniques of female principals, on the other hand, suggest greater concern for controlling the instructional process (through rules requiring lesson plans, approaches to the teaching of basic skills, and so on) and communication between teachers and parents (through rules for appropriate dress and teacher-parent conferences in the class or home).

One explanation is that the male principals studied tended to head schools serving low-income families, where they are expected to be strong disciplinarians. In this sample, 82% of the male principals were in such schools, compared to 42% of the female principals. Earlier we noted that principals in inner-city schools, regardless of sex, are most likely to promulgate bureaucratic rules for discipline. Whereas principals in lower-class schools are diverted by the problems of student disorder, those in middle and upper socioeconomic schools, mostly female, are able to concentrate their efforts on matters of instruction and relations with parents.

Age. The older principals studied (over 45 years old) were more likely to favor extensive rules for discipline (50%) and instruction (83%) than were their younger colleagues. Only one-third of the younger principals enforce these kinds of rules as religiously as older principals. Two kinds of explanations seem plausible:

—As a principal ages, he or she is likely to rely increasingly on formal rules and procedures to administer the school. As the age gap between the principal and most of the school faculty grows wider, it is more difficult for a principal to call on personal ties, friendship, and informal communication with teachers. (This explanation suggests that administrative style changes as the principal grows older. Strictly speaking, cross-sectional data, taken at the same point in time from principals of different ages, does not allow such an inference. Longitudinal data from the same cohort over time are more reliable as evidence that administrative practices of principals change as they age.)

—There may be a kind of "generation gap," in which older principals are more likely to use hierarchical patterns of leadership. In contrast, young principals have matured during an age in which public employee

unions became more militant, and when traditional areas of management prerogatives were increasingly shared with workers.

The School Faculty

Blau and Scott argue that "written procedures can become a functional
substitute for personal experience"[35] and other sorts of expertise. The
level of formal rules is greatest, they suggest, where subordinates possess
minimal expertise or social attributes conducive to the performance of
tasks. This section examines the relationship between various characteristics of the school faculty and the level of formal rules for teacher behavior.

Rate of Teacher Turnover

It was previously noted that experienced principals tend to substitute
informal channels of communication for formal rules. Similarly, one might
expect that low attrition among the faculty would encourage the use of
personal communication and reduce the importance of rules. Findings in
Table 7 display this relationship—schools with rapid teacher turnover are
likely to have a high level of formal rules for teacher behavior; conversely,
schools in which the faculty is relatively stable have fewer official procedures for discipline, instruction, and parent-teacher relations. Where faculty turnover is low, principals may rely extensively on informal patterns
of influence worked out over a period of years, or allow teachers considerable discretion in handling basic tasks.

Several factors explain why the exercise of bureaucratic authority is
more overt in schools with higher teacher turnover. As teacher and principal become more familiar with each other, teachers have more opportu-

TABLE 7. FACULTY TURNOVER AND LEVEL OF FORMAL
RULES FOR THE 31 SCHOOLS SAMPLED

| | Percent of Schools with High Level of Formal Rules for: | | | |
Faculty Turnover[a]	Discipline	Instruction	Parent-Teacher Relations	Number of Schools
Low (0-21%)	28	33	44	18
High (22-70%)	46	69	62	13

[a]Turnover rates based on 1970-1971 school year.

nity to demonstrate their abilities and, likewise, the principal acquires greater confidence that teachers will use discretion appropriately. Secondly, over a period of years of working together, teachers and principal acquire common expectations and norms about acceptable behavior. When supervisor and subordinate share similar views, they are also likely to act in ways approved by one another.

A competing explanation is that the exercise of bureaucratic authority gives rise to high teacher turnover. Those who argue that school bureaucracy thwarts talented educators will see the limitation of teacher discretion as a threat to professional authority. In such a setting, morale is low and the creative instincts of teachers are curtailed. Teacher turnover is quite natural in this kind of atmosphere. (The relationship between bureaucratic authority and teacher behavior is explored in greater depth in the next chapter.)

Teaching Experience

Organizational theorists have modified Weber's work by distinguishing between organizational authority, which is based on office, and professional authority, which is based on technical knowledge acquired through training and experience. Where teachers have invested considerable effort to upgrade their skills through education or on-the-job experience, it is hypothesized that the need for supervision is reduced. Anderson's study found that experienced teachers of science and industrial arts are subject to fewer instructional rules than are inexperienced teachers.[36] On the other hand, experience made little difference for English teachers, suggesting that the nature of the subject has a bearing on the kind of organizational control exercised. The findings in this study are quite similar—schools with inexperienced faculties (over 30% of the faculty had less than three years experience) are more likely (59%) than other schools (36%) to have extensive rules for instruction. However, total teaching experience has little bearing on rules for discipline and relations with parents. The differences stem largely from the various kinds of expertise necessary to perform these tasks.

It was previously suggested that discipline and dealing with parents are highly subjective areas of teacher behavior. In large measure, expertise depends on understanding, reputation, charisma, loyalties, and personal relationships. Unlike instruction, such traits are not easily transferred from one school situation to another. Where expertise is derived from the rapport between teacher and client, change in one of the parties means that the relationship must be cultivated anew. Although teachers

accumulate useful knowledge in the subjective art of discipline and dealing with parents, this expertise is not strictly additive as teachers move
from one school to the next.

In contrast, instruction is a more specific, limited, and technical
aspect of teacher behavior. Skills acquired in one school are more readily
applied in another setting. Thus, although teachers may change schools
several times, the instructional techniques of one school may be used
elsewhere; with extensive experience in several schools, teachers acquire
expertise in the instructional area sufficient to diminish the need for
organizational controls. Such transfer of expertise is inhibited by the personal factors involved in discipline and parent-teacher relations—hence
the finding that total teaching experience has little relationship to the
level of rules in these areas.

Although the personalistic nature of expertise means that authority
must often be reestablished when a teacher transfers from one school to
another, the authority of a teacher is sustained and grows with additional
years in the same school. Thus, new teachers have a more difficult time
"establishing authority" in the beginning of the school year than do
teachers with existing reputations for fairness, "tight" discipline, and expertise. As noted earlier, schools with high teacher turnover—where the
average length of teaching experience in the current school is brief—are
likely to have extensive rules for discipline, instruction, and parent-
teacher relations. Unlike the length of teaching experience in all schools,
years spent working in one school setting foster a cumulative expertise,
reducing the reliance on formal rules to direct teacher behavior.

These findings illustrate major limits on the scope of bureaucracy in
schools. Because so much of the teacher-client relationship occurs in
unplanned, nonrecurrent, highly personalistic circumstances, standardized bureaucratic principles are extremely difficult to define and apply.
Teacher expertise—gleaned from serious discussion and informal gossip
among colleagues, subjective judgment, and personal experience—is
often a more accurate guide to teacher behavior than formal rules. In
some areas we find that the latter don't even exist to any significant
degree.

Education of the Faculty

School systems purchase professional training by awarding salary
increases to teachers who obtain advanced academic degrees. Monetary
reward is based on the belief that post-baccalaureate education improves

the teacher's expertise. If formal rules are substitutes for expertise, schools with a high level of educational attainment among the faculty should have little need to call upon schoolwide rules for teacher behavior. This study found that schools in which few teachers possess a master's degree or equivalent (less than 12%) were twice as likely to have extensive rules for instruction (65%) and relations with parents (65%) as schools with better educated faculty. Where educational attainment is high among the faculty, one finds few rules for teacher behavior in these areas. Advanced degrees have little relationship, however, to administrative procedures regarding discipline.

It may be argued that the acquisition of advanced degrees represents a poor measure of actual teaching competence. Rather, teachers obtain graduate training to qualify for salary increments offered by the school system and to assure their continued employment. In short, advanced degrees may be a better indicator of a teacher's organizational commitment than they are of actual teaching competence. Through advanced training a teacher may acquire or demonstrate to supervisors that he or she shares the organization's premises of decision-making. In this respect, teaching experience and post-baccalaureate educational attainment work in a similar way to demonstrate commitment to the organization and mastery of its rules, thus reducing the need for overt bureaucratic controls.

Certification Status

Tenure is conferred on teachers after two years of satisfactory performance. It provides considerable job protection under the provisions of the civil service system. Like experience and education, tenure is often taken as an indicator of teaching competence. Some have suggested, however, that tenure fosters excessive teacher independence from organizational control, and a lack of accountability. By providing a high degree of job security, it is argued that teachers are exempted from responsiveness to client and supervisor.

This study found little relationship between the level of formal rules and the proportion of teachers in the school elected to tenure. Unlike experience and education, certification status has little impact on the rules of behavior that pertain to teachers. Whereas education and experience appear related to teaching skill, and thus a substitute for organizational rules, tenure status does not, because it is substantially unrelated to teaching competence in the schools studied.

Sex and Race of the Faculty

Earlier in this chapter, we noted that some personal attributes of principals, such as sex, are related to administrative practices; others, such as race, are unrelated. We also find a negligible correlation between racial composition of the faculty and the level of rules for teacher behavior. In addition, the proportion of males to females on the faculty has little relationship to the incidence of rules for discipline, instruction, and parent-teacher relations.

Conclusions

This chapter has described a complex pattern of organizational rules for teacher behavior, with considerable variation among schools and within schools, between the different tasks that teachers perform. Among the findings are:

—Schools in which students are primarily from middle- and upper-income familes frequently have extensive rules and procedures to govern relations between parents and teachers. Lower-class schools differ significantly; they have few rules in this area. On the other hand, in schools with low student achievement and high truancy, there are somewhat more rules for discipline and the maintenance of order than in schools with above average records of student achievement or school attendance.
—Older principals are inclined to exercise extensive controls over instructional procedures in their schools. Male principals and those over 45 years old also have a greater tendency to emphasize discipline rules than do younger, female principals. On the other hand, female principals are more likely than male principals to rely heavily on rules for instruction and parent-teacher relations.
—Experience as a principal seems to discourage the use of numerous rules, particularly in matters of discipline. Although older principals exercise considerable hierarchical control through organizational rules, such practices are surprisingly uncommon among experienced principals. A possible explanation for this seeming discrepancy is that, among school principals studied, age and experience are not related factors $(Q = .03)$.
—The higher the rate of faculty turnover, the greater the need for rules and procedures to control teacher behavior.
—Advanced education among faculty members reduces the reliance on

rules for instruction and parent-teacher relations, but has little bearing on rules for discipline.

—Race of the principal and racial composition of the faculty have a negligible relationship to all rules and procedures for teacher behavior. Similarly, certification status of teachers is not a factor affecting the extensiveness of rules in a school.

One interesting finding has been that schools do not put equal emphasis on rules in all areas of teacher behavior. Rules for discipline and parent-teacher relations have a strong positive association $(Q = .60)$, but there is little connection between either of these and instructional rules. This suggests that studies focusing on one area of school organization, such as instruction, are likely to provide a narrow and perhaps biased view of bureaucratic rules in other important aspects of daily school activity. In addition, it supports explanations throughout this study based on distinctions in the nature of various teaching tasks. The varied bases of teacher authority and expertise in matters of discipline, instruction, and relations with external clients, such as parents, clearly reflect the wide range of functions served by schools.

It is currently popular to describe schools as bureaucratic institutions. This chapter has examined one of the aspects of bureaucratic schooling—formal rules and regulations that direct, delimit, and proscribe everyday interaction between teacher and client. There are, of course, other aspects of school organization that might be examined, and might even lead to different conclusions—among them are rules that regulate school attendance, student progression from grade to grade, school budgets, teacher salaries, and so on. Nevertheless, the evidence in this chapter indicates a dramatically different view of school organization than is currently popular.

Significant areas of interaction between teacher and client are relatively devoid of precise rules for the conduct of everyday affairs. Subjective judgments, accumulated experience, and collegial advice are often more important than any bureaucratic rules stipulating teacher behavior. Persuasion, charisma, and personal leadership skills have not been supplanted by universal rules and impersonal decisions of bureaucrats whose knowledge of student needs may be questionable. What exists is a system that gives teachers considerable discretion, to use wisely or abuse, over everyday classroom activities. The following chapter examines the consequences of school bureaucracy, and conversely, the effects of discretion on teacher attitudes and behaviors.

IV

The Consequences of School Bureaucracy

A striking characteristic of the modern organization is its formal system of rules for the allocation of resources, authority, and basic tasks. This structure is intended to set out procedures for the efficient achievement of stated objectives. In an organization such as a school, where many of the core activities center around interpersonal relationships, the ability of bureaucratic rules to channel the energies of teachers toward desired ends is increasingly questioned; rather, many argue that such a formal system induces behavior that detracts from educational objectives. This chapter examines the relationship between bureaucratic rules for teacher behavior and key teacher attitudes. The central question is: do bureacratic rules breed conditions of organizational pathology, by introducing incentives for rigidity, conformity, ritualistic behavior, and ideologies hostile toward clients and administrators?

Max Weber regarded the discharge of business according to calculable rules as essential to objective, efficient performance of tasks.[1] Others such as Herbert Simon suggest that formal rules influence behavior toward efficiency and rationality by ordering the values and facts constituting the premises by which decisions are made.[2] In schools, therefore, organizational rules are originally intended to guide teachers to act in ways that support the educational objectives of schools.

There are several ways in which rules for teacher behavior may accomplish this purpose. Blau and Scott emphasize that a system of formally structured roles limits the range of informal interaction and the amount of deviation from organizational goals.[3] The ability of subgroups and cliques to pursue independent courses that undermine organizational effectiveness is diminished when leaders articulate expectations through the enforcement of rules. In addition to guiding behavior, rules have other functions as well. They may protect teachers from criticism by transferring responsibility for unpopular behavior to leaders who make the rules; the argument that teachers do not make the rules but simply follow them is frequently used as a defense against critics. Principals are also expected to support teachers who enforce the school rules; by suggesting that teacher behavior is rooted in organizational rules rather than personal whim, behavior of teachers acquires the aura of rationality.

Other theorists have suggested, however, that hierarchy, formal rules, and the traits associated with Weber's model of bureaucracy frequently direct behavior away from organizational goals by (a) substituting decisions based on position in a formal hierarchy for those derived from knowledge and experience, (b) adversely affecting the attitudes of those responsible for carrying out basic tasks, and (c) placing organizational interests above those of clients.

Robert Merton argues that compulsive adherence to rules characterizes bureaucracy, and results in unintended behavior contrary to organizational ends.[4] Among the attributes of bureaucratic behavior he cites are the deification of rules as ends in themselves, impersonal and categorical treatment of clients, excessive secrecy, and an inability to adjust to circumstances not anticipated by the rules. Similarly, Gouldner suggests that extensive rules foster incentives for minimum performance, apathy, and avoidance of responsibility.[5]

One of the central assumptions made by critics of bureaucracy is that subordinates truly desire to participate in the decisions normally made by management. It is argued that bureaucratic rules restrict autonomy and decision-making responsibility, thereby giving rise to dissatisfaction, poor performance, absenteeism, and other forms of dysfunctional behavior.

The assumption that subordinates seek to maximize their role in organizational decisions has been strongly challenged by Michel Crozier. In his insightful study of French bureaucracy, Crozier argues "that a bureaucratic system of organization always relies on a certain amount of compulsory participation which appears to be, under the present conditions, more gratifying for the individual than the voluntary participation for which—as is, perhaps, too readily believed—he is fighting."[6] Crozier argues that, contrary to conventional wisdom, rules serve to increase the independence and bargaining power of subordinates. Within the boundaries delimited by rules, workers are free to make extensive commitment to the organization, or to engage in behavior they find more personally rewarding. Rules also vest subordinates with power, for compliance may be bargained in exchange for special benefits.

Evidence in other studies indicates that organizational rules frequently channel behavior and attitudes toward useful ends. Bonjean and Grimes found "alienation" somewhat greater among workers in non-bureaucratic settings.[7] Similarly, Kohn's study concluded that workers in bureaucratic organizations are more likely than those in nonbureaucratic settings to exhibit self-direction, open-mindedness, a sense of personal responsibility, and receptivity to change.[8]

Anderson attempted to apply a bureaucratic model to explain teacher behavior in a sample of junior high schools. He found, contrary to his hypothesis, a negative relationship between teacher perceptions of conflicting authority and the level of bureaucratic rules for teacher behavior: where administrators established specific rules for instruction, teachers were least likely to perceive threats to their professional integrity.[9] In addition, organizational rules were unrelated to the impersonal treatment of students by teachers, or teacher resistance to innovation. A study by Moeller and Charters indicated that teachers in bureaucratic schools "had a significantly higher—not lower—sense of power in school decision-making than those in less bureaucratic systems."[10] Although these studies may be limited in that they do not use common or comparable measures of "bureaucracy," taken as a whole they question the conventional wisdom that school bureaucracy is the cause of teacher dissatisfaction, red tape, inefficiency, or serious mistreatment of clients.

Another way of looking at school administration is in terms of its nonbureaucratic character. Through design or incapacity, organizational tasks are frequently delegated to teachers by the absence of formal rules: teachers often report, for example, that they are expected to handle discipline problems on their own, without rules for appropriate behavior. Resort to higher authority is considered a sign of ineffectiveness. Such systems comprise fairly autonomous individuals, performing tasks independent of formal rules or close scrutiny.

Street-level bureaucrats, such as police and teachers, are commonly pictured as having considerable discretion over the performance of basic tasks. Police and teachers, on the beat or in self-contained classrooms, are largely isolated from their supervisors. Their physical separation diminishes the ability of administrators to monitor behavior or to ensure that subordinates will make proper decisions in "spur of the moment" crises. A key issue under these conditions is the way in which the exercise of discretion evolves into adaptive strategies consistent with organizational objectives.

An overview of these studies suggests the confusing, seemingly contradictory nature of the results. Katz and Eisenstadt suggest that over-bureaucratization and de-bureaucratization represent different views of the same phenomenon—a disturbance in the relationship between the organization and its environment.[11] Over-bureaucratization results in rigidity and inability to respond to individual needs or changing conditions; de-bureaucratization represents a vacuum in which leadership is illusory, and individuals act independently while holding nominal membership in the organization.

The following discussion examines the hypothesis that bureaucratic school organization fosters "maladaptations" of the teacher role—in which teachers come to perceive their responsibility in custodial terms, parents and principals represent threats to teacher authority, and significant educational innovations are rejected for fear of upsetting current arrangements.

Given the inconsistency of previous research, and the complex nature of school relationships, one is reluctant to categorize school organization on the basis of a single dimension; therefore, the findings in this chapter distinguish among organizational rules for discipline, instruction, and parent-teacher relations. In previous chapters we observed a relationship between forms of school organization and the socioeconomic, racial, and educational traits of clients; we also found that these client characteristics have an independent effect on teacher attitudes and behavior. In order to avoid confusing the relationship between school organization and teacher behavior, it will be necessary to statistically control these socioeconomic and educational background factors. In short, the effects of bureaucracy on teachers will be gauged by comparing otherwise similar settings—ones in which student characteristics are essentially alike.

School Rules and Custodial Orientation
Toward Pupils

The custodial orientation emphasizes subordination of pedagogical tasks to the maintenance of classroom discipline, threats to teacher authority, and a sense of pervasive disorder in the school. Teachers expressing custodial attitudes often perceive discipline as the overriding issue in the school, one that threatens the authority of school officials and may be symptomatic of broader social disarray. Ardent critics of school bureaucracy frequently regard the custodial atmosphere found in classrooms as the product of organizationally mandated rule-conformity by teachers. The findings in this study, however, depart dramatically in several areas from the conventional stereotype of bureaucratic dysfunctions. The major findings (see Table 8) follow:

—There is a negative association between the level of formal discipline rules and custodial orientation toward pupils. Where administrators "lay down the law" with respect to student discipline, teachers are least likely to express a custodial-control oriented view of teaching.
—Rules for parent-teacher relations and custodial orientation among teachers are inversely related. As before, strong guidelines from the principal seem to diminish the likelihood that teachers will seek to secure their status through restrictive custodial attitudes. The association is strongest among teachers in predominantly white schools with high student achievement, low truancy, and high parent income.

TABLE 8. FORMAL RULES AND CUSTODIAL ATTITUDES AMONG TEACHERS, CONTROLLING FOR STUDENT BODY CHARACTERISTICS (N = 220)

Student Body Characteristics	Association (Yule's Q) Between Teachers' Custodial Attitudes and Formal Rules for:		
	Discipline	Instruction	Parent-Teacher Relations
Achievement			
Low	−.10	.30	−.04
High	−.30	−.17	−.59**
Percent White			
Low	−.10	.29	.01
High	−.23	−.11	−.53**
Truancy			
High	−.19	.22	−.22
Low	−.18	−.21	−.35
Parent Income			
Low	−.27	.15	−.10
High	−.11	−.13	−.24

**$p \leq .05$

—Among teachers in schools whose clientele may be termed largely lower class and predominantly black, as the level of formal rules for instruction increases, so too does the incidence of custodial attitudes among teachers.

Formal Rules for Discipline

It is not surprising that custodial attitudes of teachers are related to administrative practices regarding discipline in the school. Several studies indicate that teacher attitudes toward students, the principal, and the school in general are closely connected to the way in which discipline problems are handled, and to the sense of administrative support in this area.[12] The negative association between discipline rules and custodial attitudes, however, contrasts with the general tone found in much organizational literature. According to Merton, one might have expected teachers in schools with a high level of disciplinary rules to express more impersonal, destructive, or arrogant feelings about pupils. The data suggest, however, that teachers in such schools are less fearful of threats to their authority, of disorder, or of the consequences of relationships with students than are teachers in schools with few rules for discipline. The explanation of this finding involves three concepts:

—The experience of dealing with discipline problems often gives rise to feelings of frustration, anxiety, and threats to authority among teachers.
—Custodial attitudes are a means of "coping" with these feelings, reducing the sense of inconsistency with other dimensions of the teaching role.
—The function of formal rules for discipline is to alleviate much of the burden upon teachers, transferring responsibility to the principal, and thereby moderating some of the tensions giving rise to custodial attitudes.

Maintaining order and discipline in the classroom involves a large measure of discretion and individual judgment on the part of the teacher. Supervisors, colleagues, perhaps even students, expect teachers to handle ordinary discipline problems on their own. For the most part, teachers feel that academic preparation is of limited value when applied to everyday crises in classroom discipline. Predictability, control, and stability derive largely from personal arrangements and style, neither of which is defined by the official teacher role or professional norms. In handling disciplinary matters, the teacher is drawn into an extensive social relationship with students, in which personalities and subjective considerations can be more important than any authority flowing from the official position of the teacher.

A high level of conflict in some classes creates among teachers a sense of isolation, ambiguity, and inadequate authority. Although the teacher is expected to maintain discipline in the classroom and prevent conflicts from spilling over into public view—in the hallway, cafeteria, on field trips, and among visitors—there is very little in his or her professional training that suggests remedies to contain conflict. In contrast, the teacher possesses a range of diagnostic techniques for instruction and cognitive development which, if utilized, fulfill expectations for adequate performance. In addition, teachers can consult with peers on matters of instruction without seeming to expose their own shortcomings.

These factors in the nature of teacher expertise are intensified by the absence of role boundaries to distinguish areas of teacher responsibility from those of parents, or of society in general. In contrast to instructional matters, where professional expertise clarifies the boundaries of authority, teachers and parents occupy overlapping roles in many matters related to the discipline, moral education, and socialization of the child. For a portion of each day, the teacher assumes responsibilities that were previously the province of parents. School prayer, for example, is one national issue in which the borderline between school and parent responsibility has been hotly disputed. Seating arrangements and restrictions on children's walking around the classroom are less dramatic areas in which parents are apt to perceive efforts to maintain order as autocratic barriers diminishing childhood curiosity. Where the boundaries of appropriate role behavior between parent, community, and school are fuzzy, teachers may become embroiled in conflicts with parents over different interpretations of each other's responsibility.[13]

In contrast to instruction, the discipline task is characterized by limited organizational authority, broad but vaguely defined professional norms regarding behavior, conflicting role expectations, and extensive personal contacts between teachers and pupils, and some parents. Although the need to maintain order in the classroom is almost always recognized, the standards that separate deviance from acceptable behavior, and the means used to curb disorder, are often matters of subjective judgment and great contention in schools.

The custodial orientation refers to attitude and behavior traits in which the dominant role of the teacher is seen in terms of the maintenance of classroom order and defense against threats to authority. It may be argued that the custodial orientation is an adaptive strategy to reduce the gap between limited authority, unavoidable pressure to handle discipline problems within the classroom, lack of professional norms, and the personal needs of teachers for some degree of predictability, control, and stability in daily relationships.

The custodial orientation offers a rudimentary philosophy for daily classroom management and a means of limiting the psychological risks posed by extensive personal involvement with clients. It suggests priorities among the various teaching functions of control, instruction, socialization, and certification. In addition, it establishes a buffer between teacher and student in which classroom conflict need not appear to be interpersonal in nature; rather, classroom conflict may be regarded as a product of the formal "adversarial" roles occupied by teachers and students.

Wilson has argued that police employ rituals and routines, categorization of clients, and informal codes of behavior as a protection against the ambiguous, discretionary, and personally threatening aspects of their responsibility to maintain order.[14] Similarly, studies in mental hospitals cite the rejection of therapeutic values, macabre jokes about patients, and obsession with organizational details as means workers use to detach themselves from personal involvement with patients.[15]

In this study, teachers in schools with extensive rules for discipline are less likely to express custodial attitudes than are teachers in schools with minimal rules in this area. Disciplinary rules serve a positive function in clarifying and formalizing expectations about this sensitive aspect of the teaching role. Katz and Kahn define a formalized role system as "one in which the rules defining the expected interdependent behavior of incumbents of system positions are explicitly formulated and sanctions are employed to enforce the rules."[16] They argue, as does Ruddock, that such rules reduce the extent of subjective, or personal, involvement in occupational roles.[17] Rules serve as guides to behavior, confer authority, and provide grounds for teachers to defend themselves against criticism. Rules may also communicate the intention of a principal to "back up" the faculty. In short, formalized rules for discipline provide the teacher with resources that reduce the sense of ambiguity, isolation, inadequate authority, and personal threat commonly found among those performing discipline tasks. In the absence of organizational rules for discipline, on the other hand, teachers are likely to employ custodial-type strategies in order to bolster authority and reduce ambiguity about the performance of discipline tasks.

Parent-Teacher Relations

In schools with extensive rules for parent-teacher relations, teachers are less likely to express custodial attitudes than are teachers in schools with few such rules. This finding is quite notable in middle-class white schools (see Table 8), where parent income and student achievement are high, and truancy rates are low. In lower-class, black schools, there is negligible correlation between rules for parent-teacher relations and custodial teacher attitudes.

Teacher relations with parents have many of the same attributes as found in the disciplinary task. Becker notes that conversations between teachers and parents most frequently dwell on the subject of discipline—usually the teacher is defending some action against criticism or seeking help from parents to curb student excesses.[18] Bowman has suggested that perhaps 90% of the criticisms of teachers arise from the manner in which discipline problems are handled.[19] Similarly, Jennings's analysis of a national sample of parent attitudes indicates that the great majority of parental grievances deal with matters other than curriculum—the style in which students are taught rather than what they are actually taught.[20] In some ways, dealing with parents is an extension of the classroom disciplinary task, characterized by vague notions of professional expertise, limited official authority, conflicting role expectations, and extensive personal involvement in face-to-face relations with parents. Although some teachers derive great satisfaction in working under these conditions, others experience a sense of inability to handle responsibilities, of disordered school relationships, and of threats to authority.

It has been argued that teachers in middle- and upper-class communities feel more threatened by parents than do those teaching in lower-class schools. The middle-class school, as noted by Sieber, Becker, and others, is often characterized by a high degree of parental participation, articulateness, and assertiveness;[21] many parents in these schools also possess professional credentials equivalent or superior to those of the teacher.

In addition to direct participation, middle- and upper-class parents are more likely than lower-class parents to engage in a form of indirect teacher observation. Checking homework and asking children about their schoolday are means of finding out about classroom activities. Through their children, parents learn a great deal about classroom practices, teaching methods, and school services. This kind of indirect observation may make some teachers feel uncomfortable; they may come to regard pupils as conduits for parental scrutiny—giving rise to custodial teacher attitudes.

Formal rules for parent-teacher relations reduce this sense of threat by defining, limiting, and specifying appropriate role behavior for teachers and parents. For example, school rules may tell a teacher when to expect parents in the classroom, and what to do if a parent's unexpected entry interrupts the lesson. Such rules remove the burden of decision-making from teachers and provide some protection against what may seem to be unreasonable demands. Thus, in middle-class schools, as the level of rules for parent-teacher relations increases, the proportion of teachers who express custodial attitudes declines.

Formal Rules for Instruction

The relationship between rules for instruction and custodial attitudes toward students offers an interesting contrast. Among teachers in inner-city schools (those schools that are low-achieving, predominantly black, and have high truancy), one finds a positive association between the level of instructional rules and custodial attitudes; in middle-class settings, however, the relationship is almost negligible.

In performing the instructional task, the teacher possesses a wide range of professional expertise obtained from college training and on-the-job experience. College courses in curriculum, planning, testing, methods, and so on provide preparation with some value for instructional behavior in the classroom. In addition, school resources such as textbooks, teacher guides, instructional materials, remedial specialists, and supervisors offer rich sources of technical assistance. These factors are reflected in public perceptions of teacher expertise. In a study of teacher roles, Biddle argues:

> Americans have come to expect that teachers both possess a college education and will meet minimal standards of certification set by the state. Thus, it is felt that teachers are a well-trained professionalized body . . . who are competent to *instruct* [emphasis added]. This contrasted with the perception of teacher performance in roles requiring social skills and group management.[22]

Instruction, in contrast to discipline, is characterized by a higher level of technology, predictability, professional expertise, organizational support, and role specificity—all of which structure the teaching process and legitimize teacher expertise in the eyes of constituents.

Authority stemming from organizational rules for instruction may conflict with other professional expectations. Teacher autonomy over classroom decisions pertaining to instruction is a strong component of professional teacher expectations. Teachers may feel that rules for instruction infringe upon areas of professional prerogative. To teachers, principals who enforce rules for instruction may appear to be more interested in orderliness than in the substance of learning, or more responsive to superiors than to the needs of faculty and students.

Adopting a custodial attitude is one means of reducing the incongruity between professional and bureaucratic role expectations. The custodial orientation can reconcile incompatible demands on teachers by subordinating instruction to maintenance of order, and by externalizing responsibility for educational deficiencies. For example, teachers may attribute classroom problems to such factors as lack of principal support, excessive administrative restrictions, lack of discipline and respect for authority among students, diversion of paper work, or political interference in schools.

The positive association between organizational rules for instruction and custodial teacher attitudes applies only to schools with low achieving, largely black, clientele. In middle-class schools, the relationship is negligible and in a negative direction. The grounds for professional-bureaucratic role conflict are stronger in low achieving, black schools because in this sample, teachers in these schools generally had a higher level of actual teaching experience (see chapter two). In middle-class schools, the relatively low level of experience among faculty members makes teachers more amenable to organizational directives. Without a strong ideological commitment to classroom autonomy, bureaucratic rules are not particularly offensive to teachers. When the years of teaching experience, a frequently mentioned aspect of professionalism, is controlled, one finds virtually no relationship between instructional rules and custodial attitudes ($Q = .03$).

Although organizational theorists have suggested a basic cleavage between the bureaucratic principles of school organization and the professional expectations of well-trained and experienced teachers, the results just discussed indicate quite a different picture. By examining varied teacher functions—discipline, instruction, and parent-teacher relations—it was shown that the interaction between organizational characteristics and custodial teacher attitudes depends largely on factors intrinsic to the particular segments of the overall teaching role. Although the evidence suggests conflict between bureaucratic rules for instruction and professional teacher expectations in this area, instruction represents a significant but nonetheless limited dimension of overall teaching responsibilities. In other areas such as discipline and relations with parents, teachers welcome active administrative intervention in classroom life, perceiving bureaucratic rules as supportive rather than restrictive, and bolstering authority instead of undermining it. In the absence of such rules, teachers are unlikely to embrace custodial attitudes. Although un-fortunate from the viewpoint of school relations with clientele, such at-titudes help teachers reduce the gap between what is expected in the way of classroom management and the resources available to accomplish such tasks.

These results clearly differ from the picture described by ardent critics of school bureaucracy. The areas in which teachers operate with minimal hierarchical direction—discipline and relations with parents—are also the ones where parents feel the greatest unease about school performance. They are also the domains in which teachers are most likely to express custodial attitudes. If clients sometimes perceive bureaucracy as impersonal and inflexible, they are just as frequently irked by feelings that school officials are inconsistent or behave on the basis of personal convenience and whim. Efforts to minimize bureaucratic forms of school organization (as they affect teachers) may address the former concern while exacerbating tensions that produce custodial attitudes among teachers. The remainder of this chapter assesses the extent to which a similar relationship prevails with respect to school bureaucracy and other teacher attitudes affecting classroom performance.

School Rules and the Use of Classroom Routines

Routines are commonly used as a means of controlling student behavior, establishing authority, and maintaining order in the classroom. Teachers frequently believe that "grooving the children" reduces the risk that dis-cipline problems will escalate into more serious threats to their own classroom control. Some would argue that routinization of classroom be-havior represents an extension of larger bureaucratic principles charac-teristic of schools as a whole. Standardization of such day-to-day classroom functions as entering and leaving the room, moving about the class, and speaking with fellow students is said to derive from a bureaucratic philosophy that emphasizes order, routines, and structure.

This study supports a different view of the relationship between bureaucratic rules for teacher behavior and the use of routines in class-room management. Surprisingly, we found that there is little association between the level of formal school-wide rules for discipline and reliance by teachers upon classroom routines. In inner-city schools, however, there is a clear tendency for centralized rules for instruction to diminish the extensive use of classroom routines by teachers. There is a negative association between the use of rules for instruction and reliance on classroom routines in inner-city schools—where student achievement is frequently low ($Q = -.38$), where truancy is commonplace ($Q = -.25$), and where students are predominantly black ($Q = -.23$) and poor ($Q = -.25$).

As previously noted, routines are often intended to control student behavior and maintain order. It seems plausible that formalized instructional procedures provide a substitute for the routines that teachers might develop on their own. Activities in the classroom become structured around required pedagogical procedures, minimizing the need for additional control routines. In short, highly structured curriculum is a less obtrusive way to control student behavior than are overt rules and routines.

Other types of bureaucratic rules do not appear to increase the routinization of teacher behavior in the classroom either. Negative associations between rules for parent-teacher relations and the use of routines by teachers, notably in low income ($Q = -.33$) and low achieving schools ($Q = -.29$), reaffirm previous findings that dysfunctional behavior may diminish with greater reliance on bureaucratic principles of school organization.

Although inner-city teachers are least attracted to heavy use of classroom routines when they can rely on appropriate school-wide rules, there does not appear to be any relationship between bureaucratic rules and routines for teachers in middle-class neighborhoods. One possible explanation rests on differences in parental expectations toward schools. The typical lower-class parent, according to Hess, tells his or her child to obey the teacher, whereas middle-class parents are more likely to emphasize learning skills.[23] This distinction is supported by Hant and Rasof, who found "the teacher in the middle income, white classroom achieves control, at least in part, through a technique not mentioned by her but reported by the children—the threat of a 'list,' presumably of those not to be promoted, on which they might be put."[24] Lower-class children were less responsive to rewards and punishments based on academic status. Sieber's work confirms this distinction: he found that as socioeconomic status of parents increases there is a shift toward preferences (among mothers) for "content-oriented" teachers and away from "control-oriented" teachers.[25] Although all parents may have generally similar expectations from schools, these studies suggest that middle-class parents emphasize instruction and learning activities, whereas the lower-class parent is more inclined to evaluate teachers in terms of order and class-room control.

Our findings indicate that, where there are minimal rules, teachers in low-income, low achievement schools use classroom routines quite heavily. By implementing routines for student behavior, the teachers in these schools, it may be argued, are responding to lower-class parents' expectations for classroom control. Where the parent-teacher relationship is regulated by school rules, however, teachers have a degree of insulation from this kind of parental expectation, and are therefore less likely to rely on classroom routines.

These findings suggest an undesirable type of teacher responsiveness to school clientele. Other researchers have noted that low SES parents evaluate teachers largely in terms of classroom control. Where relations between teachers and parents are unregulated, the typical mode of teacher behavior tries to satisfy parental expectations through the heavy use of classroom routines. Under the circumstances, such teacher behavior is rational, although few educators would consider it pedagogically sound.

School Rules and Attitudes Toward Parents

In most respects, teachers and parents share a broad common interest in the education of children. In other ways, however, they hold competing views of the role of the school: the teacher has responsibility for the class as a whole; the parent, of course, is most concerned with the individual needs of his or her particular child. This kind of situation contains the seeds of potential conflict in which (a) parents scrutinize teacher behavior for possible bias or practices that threaten the values and attitudes they have attempted to inculcate in their children, and (b) teachers solicit support from parents and seek to avoid disputes that challenge their professional judgment and authority.

Many believe that the bureaucratic nature of schools contributes to teacher-client conflict. The management of educational services through rules and procedures, it is argued, gives rise to compulsive rule-conformity; relations between teachers and parents are impersonal and teachers jealously guard their authority against potential threats from parents.

The findings in this study again contradict the conventional wisdom that bureaucracy breeds pathological teacher behavior and attitudes. In lower-class schools, as bureaucratic rules (for student discipline and relations with parents) increase, teachers are less likely to perceive parents as

TABLE 9. FORMAL RULES AND TEACHER HOSTILITY TOWARD PARENTS,
CONTROLLING FOR STUDENT BODY CHARACTERISTICS (N = 220)

Student Body Characteristics	Association (Yule's Q) Between Teacher Hostility Toward Parents and Formal Rules for:		
	Discipline	Instruction	Parent-Teacher Relations
Achievement			
Low	−.30	−.15	−.24
High	−.05	.19	−.06
Percent White			
Low	−.32	−.09	−.15
High	−.01	.09	−.17
Truancy			
High	−.31*	.05	−.28
Low	−.04	−.05	.12
Parent Income			
Low	−.37**	−.01	−.39**
High	−.09	.06	.26

*$p \leq .10$
**$p \leq .05$

disruptive, hostile, or uncooperative (see Table 9). Such hostile attitudes are expressed most frequently by teachers in the least bureaucratic schools.*

Where rules for discipline and dealing with parents are fuzzy or nonexistent, teachers are likely to perceive parents as threats to their authority, as uncooperative, or as a disruptive influence in the school. In his study of a high school, Gordon argued that, in order to maintain discipline in the classroom, teachers often have to substitute personal, affective forms of authority for impersonal organizational sanctions.[26] The teacher acquires a strong stake in protecting the investment of such personal resources from what may appear to be "outside meddling."

*In middle-class schools, rules for discipline and relations with parents have little bearing on teacher attitudes toward parents. A possible explanation is that parental pressures in these schools are likely to emphasize instructional matters rather than discipline. Instruction is an area in which teachers make strong claims to professional expertise, and are unlikely to rely on personal forms of authority. Where the investment of subjective, personal resources is low, teachers are less likely to feel threatened by parental pressure. Therefore, the presence or absence of organizational rules has little consequence for attitudes toward parents.

Rules of behavior are a means of reducing the reliance on forms of personal authority: they provide teachers with a way of handling situations in a nonaffective manner. Rules serve as rudimentary guides to behavior, bases of defense against criticism, and a means of invoking administrative support against complaints. Where formal rules for discipline and relations with parents are explicitly stated, teacher authority appears to be derived from an institutional source rather than from personal relationships with clients. The teacher, as a person, is distinguished from his or her organizational role. Conflicts may challenge the organizational role of teachers without suggesting personal culpability. The teacher is therefore less likely to perceive parents as threats to classroom hegemony.

Throughout this study, discipline rules and various teacher attitudes have been most clearly associated in schools where clients are predominantly black and lower-class, undoutedly reflecting the importance of disciplinary matters to teachers in such schools. We also found, contrary to popular stereotype, that the most bureaucratic schools are often the ones in which teacher attitudes conform closest to public standards of propriety. This observation is based on teacher attitudes toward students, parents, and the use of routines. Because the consequences of school bureaucracy are often at the center of discussions of school reform, it is also appropriate to examine the way in which teachers view various policy issues. Therefore, we assessed teacher attitudes toward parental participation and toward school innovation in general.

Attitudes Toward Parental Participation and School Innovation

An examination of Table 10 reveals again that rules for discipline are an important predictor of teacher attitudes, and that the most notable relationships occur in low SES schools. Once more, the pattern of findings differs from conventional wisdom: among teachers in predominantly black, lower-class schools, those most likely to resist parental participation and school innovation are in settings with minimal rules for discipline of students. Conversely, where the discipline task of teachers is tightly structured through hierarchical rules for behavior, teachers are more receptive to parental participation in decision-making or other school innovations.

As previously emphasized, teachers often see themselves handling disciplinary tasks in the context of diffuse and ambiguous role expectations, with limited professional and organizational sources of support.

TABLE 10. SCHOOL RULES FOR DISCIPLINE AND TEACHER RESISTANCE TO
PARENTAL PARTICIPATION IN SCHOOL DECISION-MAKING AND TO INNOVATION,
CONTROLLING FOR STUDENT BODY CHARACTERISTICS (N = 220)

| Student Body Characteristics | Association (Yule's Q) Between Discipline Rules and Teacher Resistance to: | |
	Parental Participation	School Innovation
Achievement		
Low	−.22	−.32
High	−.07	−.01
Percent White		
Low	−.22	−.43**
High	−.09	−.07
Truancy		
High	−.28	−.20
Low	−.06	−.19
Parent Income		
Low	−.18	−.24
High	−.10	−.10

**$p \leq .05$

These factors encourage the investment of personal teacher resources in defining role behavior and in developing authority relationships adequate to handle the task. The teacher acquires a personal stake in maintaining the existing pattern of social accommodations. Organizational innovation and parental participation represent potential threats to this delicately balanced arrangement.

A basic function of rules is to substitute official, impersonal criteria of decision-making for subjective, whimsical, or personal standards. In specifying behavior, rules diminish the sense of a teacher's personal liability for preserving authority relationships. The incentive to protect existing arrangements from parental participation and school innovation declines where teachers do not see a personal stake in the outcome of such changes. Rules accomplish their purpose by reducing the investment of "self," allowing the teacher to view the consequences of change from a more detached position.

TABLE 11. SCHOOL RULES FOR PARENT-TEACHER RELATIONS AND TEACHER RESISTANCE TO PARENTAL PARTICIPATION IN SCHOOL DECISION-MAKING AND TO INNOVATION, CONTROLLING FOR STUDENT BODY CHARACTERISTICS (N = 220)

Student Body Characteristics	Association (Yule's Q) Between Rules for Parent-Teacher Relations and Teacher Resistance to:	
	Parental Participation	School Innovation
Achievement		
Low	−.09	.20
High	−.08	.17
Percent White		
Low	.12	−.04
High	.05	−.39*
Truancy		
High	.02	.19
Low	−.24	.10
Parent Income		
Low	−.12	−.15
High	−.30	−.51*

*$p \leq .10$

We also found (see Table 11) that teachers in low truancy, high income schools are most inclined to resist parental participation where there are few rules governing parent-teacher relations. Likewise, teachers in largely white, high income schools have a tendency to oppose educational initiatives when their school has few rules for parent teacher relations. In schools with extensive rules in this area, teachers are more likely to be receptive to parental participation and educational reform.

The findings discussed in chapter two indicate that teachers in the largely white, high income schools are more likely than others to oppose forms of parental participation and educational innovation, regardless of administrative practices in their schools. In these schools, parents tend to actively and articulately press their educational expectations on teachers and officials. Teachers may feel that their professional automomy is threatened by parental scrutiny or school innovation. The prospect of new authority relationships is particularly disquieting, for teachers in middle-class schools derive considerable satisfaction from knowing they work in what is normally considered the "better" schools. Rules regarding parent-teacher relations may reduce this sense of threat by placing boundaries on parental activity in school matters, and structuring the kind of contact that parents and teachers have with one another. As a result, among middle-class schools, those with extensive rules for parent-teacher relations are less likely to have teachers who are resistant to parental participation and educational innovativeness than schools with minimal rules in this area.

School Rules and Teacher Attitudes Toward the Principal

In the daily activities of the school, the principal represents the basic source of organizational authority to teachers. He or she exercises control over the flow of educational resources into the classroom, mediates disputes, and sets standards for teacher behavior. The principal wields influence in evaluating teachers, encouraging or discouraging creativity, lending personal support to teachers, and perhaps interacting as senior colleague among peers. The principal may also incur the hostility of teachers were he or she to exercise authority in a manner contrary to their expectations or fail to assert authority in other ways.

It is sometimes suggested that the exercise of hierarchical authority by the principal conflicts with professional norms emphasizing teacher autonomy, collegial control, and authority based on expertise. At least one study, however, has concluded that principals are surprisingly unbureaucratic—"principals desire less rules for incumbents (teachers), less procedural specifics and less impersonality than do teachers."[27] Others argue that reaction to the administrative style of the principal ultimately depends on the degree to which teacher expectations conflict with perceptions of actual practice, regardless of the substantive content of such expections.

The relationship between organizational rules and teacher attitudes toward the principal is portrayed in Table 12. In general, the respect teachers have for the principal is greatest in schools with extensive rules for discipline. Particularly in high truancy, low-income schools, hostility toward the principal varies inversely with the extent of rules for discipline.

Becker writes that teachers expect the principal to "back them up," supporting teacher authority in situations of conflict with parents and pupils.[28] Our findings suggest that formal rules for discipline may communicate to teachers the principal's intention to "back them up." This finding is strongest in schools where the need for direct support from the principal is greatest—those in which poverty and high truancy rates run parallel with school discipline problems.

TABLE 12. SCHOOL RULES AND TEACHER HOSTILITY TOWARD THE PRINCIPAL, CONTROLLING FOR STUDENT BODY CHARACTERISTICS (N = 220)

| Student Body Characteristics | Association (Yule's Q) Between Teacher Hostility Toward the Principal and Formal Rules for: | | |
	Discipline	Instruction	Parent-Teacher Relations
Achievement			
Low	−.19	.08	−.06
High	−.18	.40*	.09
Percent White			
Low	−.14	.00	−.10
High	−.23	.46**	.12
Truancy			
High	−.29	.35	.19
Low	.01	.20	−.08
Parent Income			
Low	.33*	.32	−.09
High	.00	.19	.12

*$p \leq .10$
**$p \leq .05$

In contrast to findings about rules for discipline, there is a positive association between formal instruction rules and hostility to the principal: teachers do not like principals who mandate instructional methods, content, materials, or curriculum. It was previously suggested that teachers feel most comfortable performing the planning, testing, diagnosis, and curriculum selection that are part of the instructional role; they ordinarily expect considerable autonomy in this area. In the classroom, teachers possess a wide range of knowledge about instructional methods, gathered largely from college courses, personal observation, and printed teaching material. They tend to distinguish between instructional activity, which is perceived as a professional responsibility, and discipline, which is perceived as a necessary burden. School resources such as teaching manuals and curriculum guides supplement professional standards, removing much of the uncertainty, and lack of planning and control, associated with other areas of classroom responsibility. Teachers may perceive school rules for instruction as intrusions on their professional prerogative to determine these teaching methods.

These findings suggest that teachers value formal rules for discipline, but resent them for instruction. They perceive discipline rules as a type of control. The former may fill a void in the absence of legitimate, professional sources of authority. Instructional rules, however, raise conflicts with teacher expectations of classroom autonomy.

Conclusions

The direction of much recent social science research and school reform has been toward increasing the classroom discretion of teachers by reducing the importance of control mechanisms such as formal rules. Many of the findings in this chapter cast doubt on the notion that formal rules, a key dimension of school bureaucracy, force teachers to adopt insensitive attitudes toward clients, become hostile toward school leaders, or resist parental participation and educational innovations. Most strikingly, rules for discipline are negatively associated with various teacher attitudes termed "pathological": in schools with a high level of formal rules for discipline, teachers express more favorable attitudes toward parents, students, principal, educational reform, and parental participation; in schools with few rules for discipline, teachers feel a sense of isolation, uncertainty as to the limits of authority, and inadequate resources to handle responsibilities.

Discipline rules may meet fundamental teacher needs for structure and role clarification, particularly in lower-class schools. In the absence of such rules, there is a tendency for teachers to search for mechanisms that reduce feelings of anxiety, threat, and ambiguity; custodial attitudes and denigration of parents and principal are common. These coping devices bolster a sense of fragile authority, limit the nature of personal obligations, provide priorities for decision-making in the classroom, and deflect responsibility for the failure to meet educational objectives. Role defenses such as resistance to innovation and to parental participation are similarly triggered when there is weak school support for precarious teaching functions.

Many of the tasks teachers perform involve precarious values, in which authority is weakly legitimated by school rules or professional expertise. Activities such as discipline and dealing with parents involve precarious responsibilities for teachers; these frequently give rise to feelings of personal stress, ambiguity, and inadequate authority. Teachers may adjust attitudes toward clients by redefining the nature of the teaching role in order to reduce personal involvement, augment authority, and eliminate ambiguity. These attitude changes may be costly, however, for they deflect attention of the teacher away from legitimate educational objectives. By specifying the premises of behavior, school rules may clarify the nature of teacher responsibility over areas in which they feel vulnerable. As a result, teachers are less likely to embrace adaptive strategies that deviate from societal expectations about legitimate teacher behavior.

These findings have important implications for Merton's theory of "bureaucratic dysfunctions," as well as for the efforts of school administrators who seek to modify teacher attitudes. The thesis that bureaucratic organization generates a vicious cycle of rule-conformity, rigidity, and impersonal treatment of clients has prompted various reformers to call for the de-bureaucratization of schooling. Efforts to restructure school organization through vouchers to students, decentralization, or community control are motivated, in part, by a desire to ameliorate the "pathological" consequences of bureaucracy.

The findings in this chapter raise questions about the validity of educational assumptions underlying such reform efforts. Although specific reforms are not examined, there is a tenuous connection between bureaucratic organization of schools and the kinds of teacher attitudes toward clients so often cited as the justification for changes. Contrary to conventional expectations, the ability of teachers to interact with parents and students without conflict, and to accept pedagogical and organizational reforms, appears enhanced by the reliance upon clear and concise rules for teacher behavior in areas such as student discipline and relations with parents. Organizational strategies that enable teachers to make difficult decisions, sort out ambiguous situations, and reaffirm frequently challenged authority are often well received. Extensive school rules for teacher behavior in such circumstances are apparently compatible with teacher expectations and, therefore, a reasonably successful administrative strategy.

V

The Impact of Social and Professional Teacher Attributes

Much attention has been paid to the effect of teacher characteristics—race, sex, and social class origin—on value orientations and teacher performance. One aim of school reform in recent years has been to recruit more blacks, more men, and more people from lower-class backgrounds as teachers. Those asking for school decentralization, for example, have argued that reform of hiring and promotion policies toward these ends "can direct the public school to more humanistic purpose and performance," permit more people to participate in educational decision-making, and lead to more relevant curriculum, professional behavior, and minority group role models.[1]

One frequently emphasized theme is the conflict between the middle-class values of teachers and contrary values of largely lower-class clients. Research in this area has yielded meager results, partly because of an inadequate conception of what constitutes teaching effectiveness, and partly because such ostensibly middle-class values as punctuality, neatness, control of aggression, and avoidance of conflict are also regarded by many as essential to the cohesion and persistence of any group or classroom. After an exhaustive review of existing literature, Charters concluded that "decades of empirical research have failed to identify unequivocably the behaviors which define effective teaching, much less establish an association between such behaviors and enduring personal attributes of teachers."[2]

Other studies on teacher behavior have assessed the impact of factors such as professional training, job experience, and tenure. James Anderson found that teachers with the most experience and professional training, and those with tenure, were most resistant to innovative classroom methods.[3] However, a study by Guba, Jackson, and Bidwell indicated that "teaching experience operates to erase the particular need structure which was congruent with the press of the institution [where trained and educated] and produces a pattern that is present in all teacher groups regardless of the academic background."[4] This means that teachers with similar occupational experiences tend to share similar attitudes and values regardless of differences in social background or professional training. Despite the inconsistency of empirical findings, stereotypes persist regarding the social and professional roots of various teacher attitudes.

Controversies surrounding recruitment, selection, and tenure procedures in urban schools often focus on their failure to attract teachers from minority group sectors of the community and their incapacity to exclude teachers who are clearly hostile or indifferent toward clients. For example, it is claimed that civil service hiring procedures are insensitive to the particular educational problems of lower-class, minority communities, and fail to "weed out" teachers with racial or social class biases, personality disorders, and so on. The tenure system purportedly reinforces these earlier failures by effectively preventing the dismissal of incompetent or undesirable teachers, thereby reducing the ability of school administrators to obtain teacher compliance with school policies and programs.

Others have argued that custodial attitudes, hostility toward parents, and resistance to educational innovation are part of a larger set of ideological beliefs. Harmon Ziegler's survey of teacher attitudes (during the late 1950s and early 1960s) documented the conventional stereotype of political conservatism, personal rigidity, and allegiance to "middle-class" values.[5] Even today the average teacher is often described as being inflexible, unduly concerned with status, and conservative in political and educational values.

Many believe that teachers acquire this basic outlook from others—through prolonged exposure to colleagues and daily contacts with demoralizing classroom problems.[6] For example, the importance of asserting control and maintaining classroom order is often impressed upon new teachers—by other teachers, by the principal, and sometimes by parents and students. After a period of initial resistance to such "conventional

wisdom," pressures for conformity, or simply survival, give rise to custodial attitudes, to concern for authority, for classroom rituals and routines.
This discussion contains several implicit hypotheses: that custodial attitudes, routines, hostility toward parents and principal may be most
common among teachers whose perceived interests are served by per-
petuation of current educational practices, and those teachers are most
likely to be middle-class, to be tenured, and to have extensive teaching
experience and professional training.

Alternative theses, however, may be proposed: it is conceivable that
school recruitment and promotion policies work in the manner intended,
that they confer such benefits as tenure in such a way as to reward
demonstrated competence and desirable teacher attitudes. It is also possible, as some have suggested, that job experiences tend to outweigh
personal attributes such as race, age, and sex as determinants of teacher
behavior.

A second argument is that those teachers with "pathological" attitudes leave teaching or change schools more frequently than do others.
In the preceding chapter it was suggested that custodial attitudes and
hostility toward parents and principal are informal means of compensating
for job-related stresses—deflecting attention away from one's own
shortcomings. Heavy reliance on such adaptive strategies may mean that
the teacher is experiencing considerable difficulty handling daily classroom responsibilities. It is likely that the highest rates of turnover and
transfer also occur among those teachers who feel a strong sense of isolation, role ambiguity, frustration, and threats to authority in the classroom.
One may argue that teachers with the most experience, tenure status, and
perhaps professional training, have demonstrated a measure of competence, and are therefore least likely to embrace undesired or "pathological" attitudes.

One may also suggest that there is a system of incentives for the
reduction of "pathological" attitudes. Assume that school systems and the
public actually prefer similar kinds of teachers—ones with noncustodial
attitudes and favorable views of the principal, parents, and pupils. There
may be a conflict, however, between such teacher attitudes and other
institutional norms. For example, teachers are often urged to encourage
spontaneous self-expression by students, but they are also blamed for the
resulting situations that "get out of control." Similarly, a school may wish
to "individualize" instruction, but still demands that teachers cover the
entire curriculum for his or her grade level. Under such circumstances,
some teachers might conclude that it is more important to control stu-

dents than to motivate them, or that most school innovations are merely rhetorical gestures.

When the discrepancies between various job expectations produce too much discomfort, teachers, like others, will attempt to resolve incompatibilities. One way, of course, is to quit teaching. For those who value their jobs, however, the more typical way to resolve conflict may be to bring personal attitudes into line with organizational preferences. Teachers with a substantial career investment—evidenced by tenure status, experience, academic training, and career goals—have a strong incentive to reconcile apparent conflicts among personal, public, and organizational expectations.

Findings in this study support this general notion. We asked teachers about their career plans for the next five years. Those who intended to remain in public education as teachers or administrators, or to retire, were deemed to have a "high career commitment." Those whose intentions were unclear or who planned to leave teaching were considered to have a "low career commitment." There is a consistent trend in which teachers with little career commitment are most likely to express a range of "pathological" attitudes. Those with a stake or commitment to a teaching career are less inclined to a wide range of "pathological" orientations, including custodial attitudes, resistance to innovation, or hostility toward parents. Most notably, among the teachers with low career commitment, 70% expressed great hostility toward the school principal and 51% made extensive use of classroom routines; the corresponding figures among teachers with strong career commitment were 55% and 30%. In short, the committed teacher, be it to educaton, the job, or organization, is most likely to express the "proper" attitude.

The preceding discussion suggests alternative hypotheses about the link between teacher attributes, attitudes, and performance. This chapter examines the relationship between individual teacher characteristics— race, age, sex, education, certification status, career plans, teaching experience—and teacher attitudes bearing on classroom responsibilities.

Attitudes Toward the Principal

The role of the principal is significant for teachers in many ways—as a supervisor, source of leadership, expertise, and support. We have examined the way in which teachers perceive their principal's performance in these roles, and find that many personal attributes and attitudes of teachers are closely connected (see Table 13). Teachers who are under

35 years old, black, or nontenured, are more likely to express hostility toward the principal than are those over 35, white, or tenured. In addition, there is a tendency to express a negative opinion of the school principal among teachers without advanced academic degrees, education majors (and related disciplines), teachers with less than four years total teaching experience, or four years experience in their current school.

The finding that teaching experience and tenure status are negatively associated with hostility toward the principal suggests that schools do not as readily reward teachers who are hostile to the principal. In the same

TABLE 13. TEACHER ATTRIBUTES AND ATTITUDES TOWARD THE PRINCIPAL

Teacher Characteristic	Teachers With Hostile Attitude Toward Principal (N =220)	
	%	n
Sex		
Male	53	32
Female	61	179
Age		
35 Years or less	75	101 ***
36 or above	49	117
Race		
Black	69 ·	108 ***
White	49	94
Total Teaching Experience		
Less than four years	68	120 ***
Four or more years	50	100
Certification Status		
Tenured	54	161 ***
Nontenured	76	59
Education		
Bachelor's Degree	65	125
Advanced Degree (M.A., A.B.D.,		*
Ph.D., Ed.D.)	52	94
Areas of Specialization in College		
Education, Psychology, Sociology	61	205
Other	40	15

$*p \leq .10$
$***p \leq .01$

vein, there seems good reason for teachers with the most negative opinions of their principal to avoid making strong career commitments as teachers, or investing the time, money, and energy necessary to obtain advanced professional training. Teachers with considerable costs sunk in their career and present school setting have the most to lose, and, conversely, the greatest incentive to cultivate favorable attitudes toward the principal. For those with a marginal attachment and limited resource investment in the teaching position, the potential consequences of poor relations with the principal may be of little personal concern.

No doubt, the ways in which principals reward teachers with tenure and punish others by transfer, firing, or denial of tenure shape teachers' attitudes. One may argue that after teachers acquire tenure or experience, they develop favorable attitudes toward the principal and stop seeing him or her as a threat to their position. This change of attitude may occur precisely because the principal has rewarded the teacher with tenure or continued employment. Similarly, teachers who dislike the principal may be dissuaded by this opinion from developing strong career attachments or pursuing advanced training.

The notion that investment of personal resources in the teaching career mitigates against hostile attitudes toward the principal is apparently contradicted by one finding—college majors in education (and related disciplines) are somewhat more likely to express negative opinions about their principal than teachers specializing in fields unrelated to elementary school teaching. Although the number of non-education majors in this sample is very small, this anomalous finding could reflect the pattern that finds education majors concentrated in schools serving low-income clients. The principal may become the focal point of faculty frustrations associated with all the teaching problems typical in lower-class schools.* Where the demands on teachers exceed their capabilities, teachers may simply displace their own frustrations by imputing a sense of personal despotism to school principals charged with the exercise of leadership and authority.

We also found that black teachers are more likely than whites to express hostility toward the principal. As with college education majors, it was thought that this might be due to the concentration of blacks in the tense atmosphere of inner-city schools. However, controlling for the social class characteristics of students does not explain the difference:

*Fifty-seven percent of the college education majors (and allied disciplines) sampled are in low-income schools; 43% are in high-income schools. The extremely small number of teachers who are not education majors prevents introducing control variables, such as parent income, which would test this explanation.

TABLE 14. TEACHER RACE AND ATTITUDE TOWARD THE PRINCIPAL,
CONTROLLING FOR STUDENT BODY CHARACTERISTICS (N = 202)

Student Body Characteristics	Hostile Toward School Principal			
	Black Teachers		White Teachers	
	%	n	%	n
Achievement				
Low	65	66	53	32
High	76	42	45	62***
Percent White				
Low	63	68	52	25
High	80	40	46	69***
Truancy				
High	67	75	47	55**
Low	76	33	49	39**
Parent Income				
Low	67	72	52	44
High	75	36	44	50***

**p ≤ .05
***p ≤ .01

black teachers, regardless of school clientele, are more likely to be hostile toward the school principal than are white teachers (see Table 14). However, the most significant findings are in high achieving, largely white, low truancy, middle- and upper-income schools: here the proportion of black teachers who express hostility toward the principal is considerably greater than the number of white teachers who do so.

A possible explanation for this finding is that black teachers are more likely than are whites to feel the principal is pursuing institutional and personal career interests at the expense of teachers and students. Particularly in middle-class, largely white schools—where most of the principals are also white—as the principal pays attention to vocal parent and community groups, black teachers are especially likely to feel their interests neglected.

Custodial Attitudes and Behavior

The custodial orientation refers to a definition of the teaching role primarily in terms of the maintenance of classroom order and defense against threats to authority. It reflects an imbalance between the teacher's role of disciplinarian and that of instructor. Those expressing custodial attitudes are inclined to emphasize the permissive nature of society, the physical dangers associated with increasing discipline problems, and the need to depersonalize relations with students.

In most cases, custodial attitudes are unrelated to personal teacher attributes. The teachers most likely to express custodial attitudes toward pupils, however, are those under 35 years old ($p \leq .10$) and nontenured ($p \leq .10$). Females and blacks also exhibit a tendency to adopt custodial attitudes.

Black teachers (53%) are slightly more inclined than whites (40%) to express custodial attitudes toward pupils. This relationship is surprising, for some have argued that white teachers, particularly in ghetto schools, are prone to adopt reduced learning expectations for students, and to experience a sense of threat and conflict with "middle-class" mores.[7] Although black teachers most often work in lower-class schools, the relationship between a teacher's race and custodial attitude cannot be explained by social characteristics of the school's clientele. Findings discussed in chapter two indicate that black teachers in low achievement, black, low-income, high truancy schools express custodial attitudes more frequently than do white teachers in the same schools. It was suggested that in these schools (a) such attitudes may be tolerated among black teachers more readily than they are among white teachers, and (b) multiple difficulties confronting teachers in ghetto schools may drive out weakly motivated white teachers more often than black teachers.

We also found that a slightly higher proportion of female teachers (48%) exhibit custodial attitudes than do males (37%). Because of the small number of male elementary school teachers in this sample (32), this finding should be interpreted with appropriate caution. A possible explanation, however, is that male teachers in elementary schools are often expected to serve as authority figures. Part of this expectation includes the belief that they will be strong disciplinarians. Men accept this role, and perhaps enter teaching with more realistic expectations in this area. Female teachers, on the other hand, are likely to feel that disciplinary duties conflict with their professional role expectations. Since men are perhaps better prepared in terms of realistic role expectations to handle discipline problems, they are less likely than women to embrace custodial attitudes. This adaptive strategy, more common among women than men, is a means of reconciling competing expectations between maintaining discipline and instructional activities.

Hostility Toward Parents

This study found that teachers with a minimal investment of time, energy, and resources exhibit the greatest hostility toward the parents of their students. Younger teachers express hostility to parents (63%) more frequently than those over 35 (50%; $p \leq .10$). Inexperienced and untenured faculty display this attitude more frequently than do other teachers. Those with strong career commitments are inclined to view parents favorably; the opposite is true for teachers with weak career commitments. This pattern does not, however, extend to the way in which teachers view parents participating in school affairs. Attitudes toward parental roles in school decision-making are negligibly correlated with various personal and professional attributes of teachers: socioeconomic status of the students and the extent of the school's bureaucracy outweigh the characteristics of individual teachers as determinants of attitudes toward parental participation. (See chapters two and four.)

On the whole, the economic reward structure in schools appears to work fairly well. Teachers who view parents as supportive and cooperative are the ones most likely to be retained and given tenure. Those with the minimal investment of personal or professional career resources— either because they are young, are trained in fields other than education, or have taught for only a few years—are the greatest source of hostility toward parents. This encouraging finding may be explained in several different ways:

—Schools do indeed "weed out" those whose attitudes reflect hostility toward parents before the teacher acquires a large stake in his or her current job.
—Teachers with hostile attitudes toward parents are reluctant to invest much effort into a career where they must deal with parents so often. They are more likely to transfer schools or leave teaching entirely.
—Schools have certain institutional norms, among which are the need to accord respect to and solicit cooperation from parents. Some teachers may nevertheless perceive parents as disruptive influences, uncooperative, or threats to the teacher's position. As the personal cost of changing jobs increases (because of the time and money invested in training and job experience), so too does the incentive for teachers to modify their negative attitudes.
—Older or experienced teachers may receive greater deference from parents than younger or inexperienced teachers. In addition, because older teachers are likely to have children of school age themselves, they may be more sympathetic or tolerant of parental concerns.

We also noted the apparent vestiges of sex role difference among teachers. The study found that a somewhat higher proportion of women (59%) teachers than men (47%) express hostile attitudes toward parents. A possible interpretation is that males and females may differ in the nature of their commitment to teaching. Women have traditionally entered teaching on a short-term basis, prior to marriage and children or as a temporary income supplement. Men have been more inclined to view teaching as a permanent occupational choice, perhaps contingent upon promotion to a supervisory position but not dependent upon external family factors. Because women in the past often saw teaching as a temporary role, they may have felt less constrained than men in expressing hosility toward parents. Unfortunately, the small number of men in this sample (32) precludes introducing control variables to support this notion. Of the female teachers sampled, 55% with strong career commitment expressed hostility toward parents, whereas 68% of the weakly committed teachers did.

In the future, one might expect these sex-related differences to disappear. The elimination of institutional discrimination in policies that, for example, have required pregnant women to resign, increasing patterns of permanent female jobholding, and changes in sex-role stereotypes may significantly modify the ways in which women view their role in the education profession.

Resistance to Innovation

Anderson's study of junior high school teachers tested the relationship between several teacher characteristics and resistance to innovation. He found that sex made little difference but that "teachers with the most experience, and professional training, and those who have achieved tenure, [were] the least inclined to try new teaching techniques and curricula."[8] Although findings in this study are not statistically significant, we did find resistance to innovation most prominent among experienced teachers. Contrary to Anderson's findings, however, this study found opposition to various reforms concentrated among females and those with least advanced professional training. In addition, women, whites, and those whose college training is in education (and allied disciplines) are more likely to oppose institutional and pedagogical change than are males, blacks, and non-education majors. In contrast to Anderson's findings, this study found that certification status has little bearing on teacher attitudes toward innovation; neither does age or length of experience in one's present school.

These findings suggest that advanced academic training is positively associated with receptivity to innovation, but that teaching experience is not. Because some of the strongest proponents of educational change are in the higher academic community, teachers with extensive exposure to these circles may be more inclined to absorb and articulate this point of view than teachers with limited education. On the other hand, teachers with lengthy job experience acquire a vested interest in maintaining existing arrangements, from which they presumably derive a measure of satisfaction (as indicated by their length of employment).

White teachers (67%) are somewhat more inclined to oppose institutional and instructional changes than are blacks (56%). This finding, however, largely reflects the racial composition of students in the schools. White teachers tend to work in schools with predominantly white enrollment; in these schools, the level of resistance to innovation is greater among all teachers than it is in largely black schools (see chapter two). By comparing teachers in schools with similar racial composition, the difference between the attitudes of black and white teachers becomes negligible.

One of the interesting findings is that those whose college training has been in areas directly related to teaching—education, psychology, and sociology—are more likely to resist school innovation (62%) than those trained in other fields (47%). Although the reliability of the finding is tempered by the small number of elementary school teachers trained in other fields, such as math, science, or history, it nevertheless suggests that those most exposed to our teacher training institutions are also most resistant to new educational concepts. Those trained in unrelated fields come to teaching with few preconceptions, and appear more willing to try out new ideas for institution and school organization.

Conclusions

Much evidence in this chapter is inconsistent with the argument that institutional and social processes in urban schools foster and protect pathological attitudes among teachers. Many findings suggest that there exist incentives for teachers to cultivate attitudes consistent with public expectations about schools and institutional norms for effective teaching.

For example, teachers with tenure status seem less likely than untenured faculty to express hostility toward the principal and parents, and custodial attitudes toward pupils, and to rely on many classroom routines. Similar findings apply for teachers with four or more years experience and those with strong commitment to teaching. Another teacher attribute rewarded by schools is advanced academic course work. This study found that teachers with postgraduate degrees are more likely than those without advanced degrees to express favorable views of parents, pupils, and school innovation.

Other findings indicate that white teachers are more prone to hostility toward parents and school innovation than are blacks. These findings are counterbalanced by the greater tendency of black teachers to exhibit custodial attitudes toward students and negative views of the principal.

The overarching theme in this chapter is that tangible rewards conferred by schools—such as tenure, employment, and salary increases for advanced degrees—go least frequently to teachers expressing hostility toward the principal and parents or custodial attitudes toward the pupils. The methodological limits of this study prevent us from attributing the pattern to any one of several possible explanations:

—The selection-out of teachers with these undesirable attitudes.
—Voluntary transfer or resignation of such teachers.
—Cultivation of desired attitudes by teachers who wish to acquire or protect their job benefits.

These findings do not, of course, suggest that recruitment, selection, and retention decisions are as effective as one might desire. Critics may still argue that there is a long way to go, and that the findings in this chapter merely reflect marginal differences between teachers. The extreme difficulty of devising reliable mechanisms to select, retain, or "weed out" teachers is quite apparent. On the basis of this analysis, however, there is evidence to suggest that the procedures presently employed accomplish their purpose at least in part.

Throughout this chapter there is a consistent finding that teachers with a large occupational stake—the highly committed, those with tenure or considerable career training, or those whose years of employment have foreclosed other opportunities—are most likely to express favorable attitudes toward pupils, parents, and principal. Conversely, teachers with little stake—the uncommitted, young, untenured, and inexperienced— are more likely to harbor a range of "pathological" attitudes. One conclusion is that the current reward structure for teachers actually achieves useful objectives, but to a limited degree. These findings also suggest additional opportunities to encourage the cultivation of favorable teacher attitudes through active manipulation of rewards for excellent performance and sanctions for poor classroom performance.

At present, rewards such as tenure and employment may eliminate the most glaring incompetents. They fail to differentiate, however, between excellent and merely adequate teachers. Accountability systems should pay dividends when they employ varied salary schedules and several forms of tenure reflecting degrees of teacher competence. Although this is not the place to resolve obvious problems with teacher accountability—avoiding penalties against teachers assigned the most difficult schools and classes, discouraging risk-taking or unorthodox behavior, or establishing appropriate standards for judging performance— the evidence in this chapter should encourage further efforts to resolve these dilemmas. Although the current reward system for public school teachers accomplishes its objectives in part, additional differentiation of the reward structure should encourage teachers to further reduce the gap between appropriate and actual behavior.

VI

Delivering Education: The Politics of Implementation

Political scientists have long been concerned with the problem of educational change, both because of its intrinsic importance to most citizens and as a barometer of government services. Their research, however, has focused primarily on the behavior of educational leaders—school boards, superintendents, and interest groups. This has several consequences. First, because political scientists focus primarily on school-system leadership, they are better able to describe decision-making than to trace its impact on everyday classroom behavior. Second, theoretical and practical distortions arise because interpretations give greater emphasis to the adoption of innovations than to their successful or unsuccessful implementation.

The focus of this study is on classroom teachers, and, specifically, those aspects of the school's internal organization and relations with clientele that affect attitudes toward daily performance. Despite the traditional focus on high level decision-makers and dramatic school conflicts that periodically capture the headlines, the perspective in this study is appropriate for an analysis of school politics. The way in which citizens perceive the delivery of educational services is largely in terms of their

interactions with teachers and other neighborhood school officials. Such
interactions may shape still larger views of the political process as a whole.

This chapter will link both perspectives—the one that looks at
teachers and the one that examines high level decision-makers—
considering in particular one largely neglected aspect of educational policy: the way in which leaders interact with teachers to implement innovative educational programs and policies. Implementation, broadly defined,
refers to the process by which new programs and policies work their way
through layers of federal, state, and local authority, and are successfully,
or unsuccessfully, translated into changes in patterns of behavior at the
classroom level. For purposes of this discussion, implementation of innovations does not include the effort of individual teachers to develop special programs and materials exclusively for their own use. Our basic concern is to apply the findings of earlier chapters to the problems decision-
makers confront in attempting to translate new policies into actual practice.

Varieties of Teacher Behavior

The theme that emerges from the preceding analysis is that the teacher is
the focal point in a network of relationships with major responsibility for
orchestrating the delivery of educational service, and for conveying a
sense of school purpose to other members of the system, notably parents
and students. The process of daily communication among them contains
points of stress at which incompatible roles, extravagant expectations, and
limited predictability and control often give rise to conflict, instability,
and deviation from educational objectives. Certain aspects of the teaching
role are subject to greater stress than others; these are points at which
teachers are particularly vulnerable to claims of improper behavior, bias,
or incompetence. Other aspects of the teaching role, notably instruction
of students, are surrounded by authoritative values—accepted social
objectives, professional competence, and technical expertise—that
vest teacher behavior with an aura of legitimacy.

A major source of stress for teachers is the responsibility for discipline and maintaining order. As part of the amorphous school function of
inculcating desirable social values and behavior patterns in students, the
discipline task involves a large measure of subjective decision-making and
moral judgment. As Charles Silberman wrote, "children are taught a host
of lessons about values, ethics, morality, character and conduct every day
of the week, less by the content of curriculum than by the ways schools
are organized, the way teachers and parents behave, the way they talk to

children and to each other, the kinds of behavior they approve or reward, and the kinds they disapprove or punish."[1]

The social norms that structure achievement and propriety in family, work, and political settings are partly acquired in schools. Such learning, Dreeben argues, forms a link between school, family, and the public institutions of adult life.[2] The development of these values and attitudes is related to experiences shaped by structural properties of schools—authority relationships, activities, and sanctions—rather than a direct result of specific instructional problems.

Controls placed on student behavior through the maintenance of classroom order are one way in which the school experience transmits values and attitudes. Discipline is an aspect of the teaching task imbedded in personal values regarding morality and propriety. In this area, attempts of teachers to validate authority, claim expertise, or secure organizational resources are carefully scrutinized and frequently challenged.

The moral dimensions of schooling have a low degree of public acceptability or legitimacy. Responsibility in this area is commonly shared with other groups, notably family and church. The fuzzy boundary between the discipline task of teachers and the overall parental concern for moral education is a frequent point of conflict for teachers. Failing to carve out a clear role in this area, they often attempt to assign others as much responsibility as possible, attributing school disorder, for example, to breakdowns in family stability.

A major source of stress surrounding discipline is the lack of conventional mechanisms for validating authority—professional training, knowledge, or organizational support. Educational "software," such as books, curriculum guides, and instructional packages, reinforce authority in areas with specific, definable, secular kinds of objectives. Premises underlying teacher behavior in the area of discipline are difficult to disassociate, however, from subjective and moralistic overtones. The absence of prescriptive organizational or professional norms draws teachers into a web of affective relationships with students. As the subjective determination of behavior increases, so too does the opportunity for teachers to view disorder and conflict as personally threatening. In the absence of organizational or professional guides to behavior, evaluation of teacher performance by supervisors, colleagues, and parents is largely divorced from actual teacher behavior. Standards of competence are keyed to the demonstration of classroom control rather than adherence to authoritative norms for teacher behavior.

This discussion suggests that the paradox of the teaching role is that authoritative teacher resources are least available for precisely those tasks that are most precarious. The scope of teacher discretion and responsibility for student behavior is greatest over matters in which teachers possess the least adequate training, capacity to plan, or control events. Consequently, teachers are particularly vulnerable to feelings of isolation and lack of control over the classroom situation.

A stable system of school relationships is one that is capable of reducing conflict to manageable proportions. This study suggests that schools respond at points of greatest stress by invoking rules for the behavior of teachers. Schools with high rates of truancy are more likely to have extensive rules for student discipline than are schools with low rates of truancy. Similarly, there is a negative association between levels of student achievement, parent income, and the incidence of discipline rules.

Another source of stress is contact between teachers and parents. Where parents are articulate and assertive, as is most common in middle-class schools, teachers are likely to feel an infringement on professional autonomy. This study found that 77% of the middle- and upper-income schools adopted extensive rules for parent-teacher relations, whereas only 33% of the low-income schools did so.

The purpose of rules is to guide behavior, specify the basis for decision-making, and limit the scope of responsibility. In addition to reducing sources of role ambiguity, rules augment teacher resources in areas of precarious authority. By substituting organizational rules for the exercise of discretion, much of the affective basis underlying teacher behavior is diminished. Consequently, teachers are less likely to perceive conflict as a personal threat.

The usefulness of rules clearly depends on the nature of teacher expectations in the areas to which the rules are directed. As seen in earlier findings, teachers expect considerable autonomy over matters of instruction, for here they can claim professional expertise; teachers are likely to regard such rules as a form of interference or as heavy-handed paternalism. In matters of precarious teacher authority—discipline and dealing with parents—teachers are likely to welcome rules to limit their responsibility and shift the decision-making burden to supervisors.

Frequently, teachers desire more rules, procedures, and specificity of behavior than administrators are willing or able to provide. Under these circumstances, this study suggests, teachers are likely to embrace adaptive strategies of their own design. One may argue that the heavy use of routines, custodial attitudes, hostility toward parents and principal, represent informal attempts to depersonalize relationships and reduce teacher liability in situations of stress. Resistance to parental participation and educational innovation may similarly stem from the desire to avoid new sources of pressure and responsibility. At these points of stress, teachers are particularly vulnerable to claims of usurping authority, indifference to clients, bias, and lack of accountability and responsiveness. Such perceptions of the manner in which educational services are delivered contain the fuel for a self-perpetuating level of tension and conflict in urban schools.

Innovation: Distinguishing Between Adoption and Implementation

In the past two decades, the problems of educational reform have received greater attention from federal, state, and local policy-makers. Educational initiatives have been undertaken to meet perceived challenges from foreign enemies and societal obligations to the underprivileged, or to fend off criticism from powerful lobbies and interest groups.

Educational research has also given considerable attention to issues of school change, innovation, and the use of research and development findings. One enduring school of thought, which spans Waller's work in the early 1930s, Ziegler's mid-1960s study of teachers' political attitudes, and Gittell's contemporary analysis of urban school conflict, has portrayed schools as essentially traditional, conservative, and organized to thwart external pressures for change.[3] To some extent, many school reformers hold similar views—schools are perceived as static institutions wedded to outmoded practices because of limited resources and local control of schools by provincially minded citizens, or because school personnel are more concerned with preserving their entrenched self-interests than in educational improvement.

A competing perspective has been introduced by those who have studied the diffusion of innovations among school districts. Ronald Havelock's national survey, done in 1973, reported an apparently high level of school system "innovativeness." Self-reports from 353 school districts indicated that, during the 1970-1971 school year, each district averaged approximately nine "innovations," and that these "innovations" were accompanied by a high level of enthusiasm among respondents.[4] Although Havelock's survey is very limited—it is based on self-reports of school officials, does not assess actual practice, and treats innovation as a generic concept—it nevertheless appears that schools are constantly attempting change in such areas as curriculum, technology, organization, and personnel.

Optimistic findings such as these, however, contrast with growing evidence that a large proportion of seemingly worthwhile educational innovations ultimately fail. They may fail because they are abandoned by school officials, have negligible impact on day-to-day school practice, or are viewed less favorably by teachers, parents, principals, and students than they are by central school district decision-makers.

Although schools appear to undertake more widespread organizational and pedagogical reform than is commonly thought, relatively few significant innovations are successfully implemented and maintained beyond an initial trial period.[5] In a 1970 study, Goodlad observed a large gap between claims that innovations had been adopted and their translation into actual practice:

> A very subjective but nonetheless general impression of those who gathered and those who studied the data was that some of the highly recommended and publicized innovations of the past decade or so were dimly conceived and, at best, partially implemented in the schools. . . . [Teachers and principals] claimed individualization of instruction, use of a wide range of instructional materials, a sense of purpose, group process, and inductive or discovery methods when our records showed little or no evidence of them.[6]

It is increasingly apparent that the failure of many educational innovations may be attributed to ineffective implementation rather than to defects in the ideas or programs themselves. A number of plausible reasons have been advanced to explain the brief life of many innovations—inadequate resources, separation of research and development from actual practice, unanticipated opposition, poor planning, vague and extravagant claims of effectiveness. Lukas's review of the Head Start Planned Variation effort indicates a pattern of only partial program implementation, despite the controlled atmosphere of a quasi-experiment.[7]

Even carefully evaluated school interventions frequently flounder in "real world" circumstances unforeseen during prior stages of development and field testing in controlled settings. Many of these "real world" conditions have previously been discussed. They include the uncertainty that surrounds aspects of the teaching role, perceived threats to authority, and organizational settings that exacerbate ambiguity and leave teachers vulnerable to claims of bias, incompetence, or impropriety.

Thus, a major explanation for the discrepancy between high rates of adoption of innovations and substantially less actual change in daily practice lies in the processes by which planned changes are implemented. Most studies of school innovation focus on the means by which school authorities decide to adopt new practices in areas such as curriculum, personnel, governance, or technology. Issues of implementation, however, deal with the subsequent practices, events, and conditions under which new initiatives are successfully or unsuccessfully translated into day-to-day educational practice. From one point of view, high rates of initial innovation followed by frequent abandonment represents a healthy search for new techniques; an equally likely consequence, however, is wasteful expenditures, inflated expectations, and diminished legitimacy for school reform.

Models of the Innovating Process

The literature on educational change is dominated by assumptions about the rational manner in which school systems adopt innovations. Ronald Havelock has outlined several models sharing this perspective.[8] These are listed below:

—*Problem Solving Model:* the diagnosis of user needs conditions the selection and adoption of an innovation strategy.
—*Social Interaction Model:* diffusion of information about the presumed advantages of an innovation provides the motivation to adapt.
—*Research and Development Model:* this model lays out a linear sequence of research, development, evaluation, and dissemination activities. As in the previous models, needs assessment and the diffusion of information play a role.
—*Linkage Model:* synthesis of preceding models, it also deals with individual and organizational incentives for change. As in the previous models, the issue of change is viewed primarily in terms of the adoption of innovations.

Underlying each of the above alternatives is a view of rational behavior in which school systems establish goals, assess resources, identify target groups, and select the most efficient alternative from among those generated by research and development. It assumes that ideas, programs, or products, once proved and made known, will be recognized and used by school personnel. The prominence accorded rationality in this model of school-system innovation may be questioned on several grounds.

—It is difficult for schools to articulate a consistent set of educational priorities. The many aims of schooling are often unclear or in conflict, and among different groups there is rarely any consensus about priorities. There are many such conflicts for teachers. Efforts to "individualize" instruction, for example, involve risks that classes will appear chaotic to observers, or that parents will perceive favoritism or bias in any effort to segment the class.
—Schools may be unable to select alternatives that maximize desired

results and minimize negative consequences. Because evaluations are often absent or unpersuasive, Pincus notes, "we are often unsure whether one method of providing school services is consistently better in terms of output effects, however defined, than any other method."[9]
—Schools may be unable to harness economic resources to implement selected innovations. Some programs end when their budgets are cut. School administrators typically regard federal funds for new initiatives as "soft money," to be used when available but likely to disappear as federal priorities shift. In other cases, available resources are not utilized. During the 1973-1974 school year, the Washington, D.C., school system failed to spend $22 million in federal grants, despite a $10 million deficit in its own local budget.[10]
—Because schools are largely public monopolies, there may be little incentive to implement innovations that would maximize efficiency. Unlike private organizations, which are dependent on the marketplace for survival and allocate their resources to maximize profits, public schools ultimately depend on the political process. They are governed by elected or appointed boards, derive their income from taxes, and, because educational outputs are difficult to calculate (unlike profits), allocate their resources largely on the basis of the previous year's budget.

Decision-making in schools departs from rationality in ways quite similar to practices in other areas of public policy. Graham Allison's account of the Cuban missile crisis and David Halberstam's portrayal of American involvement in Vietnam describe the way in which bureaucratic and personal competition may cloud the consideration of alternatives, and impinge upon objectivity in national security decision-making.[11] In education, where crises are never as dramatic or as consequential as a missile confrontation or a major war, models of rationality give insufficient weight to the social and bureaucratic interests, attitudes, values, and organizational practices that affect adoption and successful implementation.

A significant aspect of school decision-making is determined by administrative practices that structure relationships among teachers, pupils, parents, and principal. Rules of behavior for teachers are an important component of the way in which school bureaucracy handles basic tasks, the manner in which teachers come to perceive their responsibilities in the classroom, and the capacity of schools to implement innovations from the "top down" or to stimulate creativity from the "bottom up."

This study revealed a pattern in which the kind of tasks to which rules applied and the differences in teachers' expectations from one task to another, determine the effect of rules on teachers' attitudes and, probably, their behavior as well. The findings suggest that teachers expect a strong degree of direction, hierarchical control, and specificity in areas such as discipline and dealing with parents. In addition to guiding behavior and protecting teachers from what may seem to be unfair criticism, rules constitute a symbol of authority and administrative support. In matters of instruction, attitudes of teachers are conditioned by a quite different set of expectations. Autonomy over the selection of appropriate teaching methods, materials, and objectives is of paramount concern. Rules for behavior are often seen as infringing on professional prerogatives regarded as properly belonging to teachers.

Policy-making is not simply limited by personal and organizational factors. Officials must still contend with the limits of rationality. Herbert Simon writes:

> The capacity of the human mind for formulating and solving complex problems is very small compared with the size of the problems whose solution is required for objectively rational behavior in the real world—or even for a reasonable approximation to such objective rationality.[12]

In practice, most complex decisions are made under conditions of risk or uncertainty. Decisions involving risk may be defined as those conditions under which the desirability of various outcomes is unknown and in which the likelihood of any alternative leading to an intended outcome cannot be predicted. Although most organizations shield their lower-level employees from uncertainty through rules for behavior, teachers, police, and other public servants have considerable discretion over significant aspects of their performance, often with undesirable consequences.

Once schools decide to adopt new policies or programs, difficulties in implementation may be related to the risky nature of such change. Several propositions may be advanced about sources of uncertainty and its likely consequences:

• Educational innovation involves departure from past practice. Such change holds uncertain consequences for individuals and organizations seeking to understand, predict, and control their environment. The degree of uncertainty is partly a function of the disparity between current practice and the projected change. It stems from difficulties in reconciling competing priorities and objectives (decorum or spontaneity, discipline or instruction) and incomplete knowledge about the consequences of a significant change (community control).

  • School systems and their personnel have limited, although varying, thresholds of tolerance for uncertainty. Apprehension arises because innovations may represent a potential threat to organizational objectives and roles, professional, institutional, and personal needs for status protection and self-maintenance. The receptivity of teachers to innovation varies from school to school, and may often reflect such factors as the socioeconomic status of the students' families, the organizational structure that helps define appropriate teacher behavior, and the attributes of individual teachers, notably experience and training. In this study we found that opposition to innovation is greatest among teachers in middle-class settings, in schools where there are few bureaucratic mechanisms to assist teachers, and among teachers for whom the uncertainty of change poses the greatest threat—because all three groups have invested heavily in teaching careers. The latter includes older teachers, those with many years of experience, and those trained in the field of education.

  • In the absence of complete knowledge about the effects of a particular innovation, new policies and practices involve risk-taking behavior. In addition to the individuals involved, the level of risk associated with change varies with the nature of the innovation and procedures for its implementation. For example, when an innovation is divisible into incremental components (training), compatible with existing values (better reading curriculum), and/or simple and cheap to implement (some kind of technology), one may predict a relatively low level of risk for the parties involved. Conversely, resistance is likely to escalate over innovations that can only occur through dramatic realignment of current relationships (community control), substitution of new objectives for previously venerated ones (the Supreme Court decision prohibiting school prayer), and/or are costly and complex to implement (teacher accountability).

  • Schools that can reduce the level of uncertainty associated with change are more likely to successfully implement an innovation than schools unable to reduce uncertainty. Some methods of risk reduction involve careful planning, persuasion, training in new behavior, shared decision-making, use of authority, cooptation of opponents, incremental implementation, and the diffusion of information.

  • Schools typically try to reduce uncertainty by responding affirmatively to those pressures for change that preserve organizational and professional prerogatives and maintain their control over the flow of resources and their monopoly of claims to authority and expertise. Attempts to regulate uncertainty in this manner, however, may result in selective adoption of cosmetic changes, sidetracking what some observers perceive as more significant innovations.

• Educational products are more readily implemented than are innovative strategies that focus on extensive behavior changes. Audio-visual materials, reading aids, curriculum products, and foreign language laboratories, for example, are more easily adopted than are ungraded classes, academic credit for non-school work experience, and differentiated staffing. In a 1974 study of "innovativeness," John De Arman questioned 2,400 high school principals.[13] Of the 33 "innovations" assessed by the study, the use of data-processing equipment was implemented more frequently than any other type of innovation. Schools were least likely to attempt such "innovations" as the 12-month school year, optional class attendance, differentiated staffing, and "school-within-a-school" programs. Educational products and technology are more easily implemented because, as noted by Berman and McLaughlin,[14] they tend to be characterized by clear goals, specific treatment, an obvious relationship between treatment and outcomes, a high probability of successful results, and focus on individuals as the units of adoption.

• The language of innovation may be more appealing than the complexities of translating rhetoric into successful practice. In education, grand verbiage is endemic to discussions of change. Sometimes such rhetoric is sufficient to satisfy interest groups pressing for reform. In his study of northern school desegregation, Robert Crain observed that controversy often ended with school boards' accepting the principle of school desegregation, despite the absence of substantive change in practice.[15]

Implementation Strategies

Barriers to successful implementation are often related to uncertainties facing those expected to engage in new patterns of behavior. Efforts to implement change may be viewed, at least in part, as attempts to reduce these risks. In this section, several approaches will be discussed, and the problems associated with each examined.

Theoretical models of change often begin with a planning phase. During this period, a deliberate effort is made to establish objectives, assess available resources in the light of program goals, outline alternatives, and specify the actions necessary to implement objectives. Effective planning prior to implementation is thought to be one way to reduce risks associated with purposeful school change. It may be the basis for anticipating problems that can arise and specifying ahead of time the kinds of behavior expected under various contingencies.

The planning process takes a variety of forms and functions. Some educational planners may focus on the components and activities that make up specific programs, whereas others are more oriented to the political process, concentrating on the cultivation of constituencies and lobbying with important decision-makers. Some planning activities may simply identify needs and objectives and provide a rationale for a particular intervention, whereas others are tied directly to management of programs on a daily basis.

Regardless of the form planning takes, there are several factors that frequently limit its impact on school policy: the short-term focus of decisions in schools, the organizational weaknesses of school planners, and the frequent failure of the planning process to culminate at a time when decisions can be made. Where decision-makers are under pressure to act vigorously, planning may appear to be a timid, evasive response to pressures for change. A related problem is that the time schedule for planning may not coincide with the schedule for decision-making. The opportunity to have an impact on school affairs is diminished when planners present their recommendations after budgets have been formulated and approved and major program decisions made for the forthcoming school year. Lastly, planners are often tenuously connected to the authority structure in school systems. Control over budget allocations, instructional activities, and program decisions are typically in the hands of other organizational units.

Even the most ardent advocates of particular innovations usually describe their successful implementation as an incremental process. "Such change often results from the accumulation of many small, undramatic modifications that individually hardly seem worth scientific scrutiny."[16] Incremental implementation is a mode of reducing the risks associated with change. By stretching the implementation phase over a long period, uncertainty associated with successive changes in behavior at any particular point in time is thereby reduced. Decision-makers have the opportunity to commit resources gradually and can more easily withdraw if mistakes are made; school personnel can adjust to new arrangements, resources and supplies can be secured to support new activities, and individuals can be trained in various roles.

There are several potential dangers associated with incremental implementation, however. First, the longer it takes to install an innovation, the more likely that there will arise changes in the logic, facts, or conditions that initially made an innovation appealing. Old coalitions of supporters break down and new alliances form, new innovations gain popularity and drain off vital resources.

Second, the sources of financial support for innovations are often unstable. Much of the financial support to undertake new programs comes initially from federal funds. Because federal agencies must justify their own expenditures to secure continued and increased funding from Congress and the administration, agencies are under pressure to demonstrate quick and visible results. Premature evaluation of incrementally implemented projects may yield disappointing results and risk loss of funding; hastily implemented programs may appear mismanaged or chaotic; and incremental implementation may result in such frequent adaptations that the original purpose or idea is unrecognizable in the final product.

A third mechanism to reduce the risks related to implementation involves shared decision-making. Administrators are frequently exhorted to use such vehicles as teacher advisory committees and blue ribbon commissions, or to consult with teacher union representatives prior to final decisions. Likewise, educational researchers and developers are encouraged to regard the users, typically teachers and students, as active recipients of products and plans, and to include such groups during prior stages of planning and development.

The role played by interest groups, opinion leaders, community residents, and school staff at various stages in the planning and implementation of innovations may exercise a significant influence on the ultimate outcome of attempted changes. Selznick's study of the TVA demonstrates how early involvement of potential opponents—private industry and farmers—greatly reduced subsequent conflict.[17] The nature and extent of participation in decision-making is a means of reducing the risks associated with innovation by giving potential sources of opposition a stake in the outcome, by spreading responsibility for the consequences, adverse or otherwise, among several groups, by increasing knowledge about the consequences of change, and by bringing diverse sources of expertise to the decision-making process.

The efficacy of implementation strategies that spread decision-making responsibility assumes that users, notably teachers, wish to participate in making decisions that affect their classroom behavior. This may not always be the case, for the uncertainties associated with innovative behavior may be outweighed by the risks of sharing responsibility for the decision itself: the former simply requires that teachers comply with decisions that are made, but the latter implies culpability for undesirable consequences.

The desire to participate in decision-making is selective. Teachers and their unions wish to influence decisions on the economic conditions of employment and resist incursions on teacher discretion in their areas of expertise, notably instruction of students. This study has observed that teachers welcome the opportunity to withdraw from a decision-making role in areas of discipline and relations with parents. When teachers are particularly vulnerable to claims of bias, impropriety, or incompetence, they desire bureaucratic rules that provide hierarchical control and direction. In the absence of such rules, teachers are likely to regard the principal as unsupportive, to routinize behavior in the classroom, and to adopt negative views of students and parents. By substituting organizational rules for teacher discretion, teachers shoulder less decision-making responsibility, particularly over matters in which their expertise is often challenged, and, consequently, their authority is precarious.

Michel Crozier has observed situations in other organizations that lead individuals to retreat from a decision-making role:

> Confronted with an over-demanding situation with no expectation of significant reward, individuals will choose to reduce their involvement and to commit themselves as little as possible to the organization. The pattern of impersonality and centralization brings great pressure in this direction. On the other hand, it deprives people of the possibility of personally influencing decision-making, and thus precludes any hope of recognition. On the other hand, it does not demand anything but formal compliance from individuals. People are not invited to participate, and, if they retreat, they risk little punishment.[18]

Although planning, shared decision-making, dissemination of information, and staff training are useful means to mobilize support and capability for implementation, the backbone of schools, like that of most organizations, rests upon formal authority to direct the behavior of its members. Some have argued that the modern school organization relies excessively on bureaucratic authority as a basis of controlling teacher behavior, and, by encouraging ritualistic adherence to formal rules, such control mechanisms often work to impede educational change.

In the current study, however, it was suggested that significant areas of teacher behavior, particularly student discipline and relations with parents, are relatively unbureaucratic—teachers are largely independent operators, often subject to general expectations but rarely guided by specific rules for behavior and decision-making. The study also indicates that organizational authority and rules for teacher behavior may be a useful means of reducing the risks associated with educational change by:

—Specifying exact behavior from teachers.
—Conferring authority on those who must implement an innovation.

—Limiting possible deviation from the objectives of new initiatives.
—Abstracting teachers from personal responsibility for the ineffectiveness or unanticipated consequences resulting from implementation of an innovation.

Research Needs

Studies of adoption dominate the literature on educational change. The relative handful of studies on implementation issues are typically anecdotal "show and tell" accounts of a local effort to implement curriculum change in a small number of schools.[19] These studies have a marked tendency to explain observations in idiosyncratic terms—the presence or absence of a dynamic, dedicated leader being the most important determinant of successful implementation. Their findings rarely treat systematic patterns of organizational behavior, decision-making, and institutional incentives for change.

There are several reasons why implementation is one of the major unexplored areas of educational change. To begin with, it is costly and time-consuming. Data must be collected from people at several levels—including superintendents, principals, teachers, and perhaps even students. It may take months or years to establish adequate rapport with school personnel in central, regional, and local headquarters, or in the schools in which implementation is taking place.

Second, implementation is not of primary interest to those who might fund such research. Commercial publishers marketing many of the new products are predominantly interested in decisions about adoption of their texts and materials. There is little concern for the subsequent use of such products. There is also a tendency for federal agencies to subsidize research that emphasizes the self-reported adoption of innovations. Long-term analysis of implementation is neglected because it is unlikely to provide the short-term, visible, and preferably positive results that agencies would like to report to Congress and constituents.

Another reason is that money for evaluation is ordinarily scarce. When and if the effects of an innovation are assessed, it usually occurs during latter stages of development, preferably in a controlled experimental setting. Research on the effectiveness of innovations once implemented in the "real world" is rarely undertaken.

There is little research on implementation because it is costly, of minor interest to commercial sources, and does not promise to yield short-term visible results to federal funding agencies. Consequently, discussions of implementation are largely atheoretical and borrow heavily from other fields, notably organization theory, research on the dissemination of agricultural innovations, and educational research and development. The educational research undertaken is often retrospective and flows from the belated recognition that innovations encounter organizational and political obstacles foreign to the carefully controlled, somewhat artificial laboratory setting.

Several recommendations for improving implementation may be suggested:

—Evaluations should be of sufficient duration to determine if effectiveness "holds up" once products are implemented.
—Research on school system "innovativeness" should extend beyond central decision-makers—superintendents, chief administrators, and principals. Research should encompass several hierarchical levels, and trace the process that links innovative ideas to daily practice.
—Comparative studies of implementation should be undertaken. Small scale case studies, although useful, give rise to idiosyncratic explanations heavily weighted to personal qualities of the leadership. In addition, it is difficult for the findings to separate the effectiveness of a particular implementation strategy from the intrinsic appeal of the innovation itself.
—Studies should be accompanied by explicit definitions of the term "implementation," more realistic criteria and improved measures of successful and unsuccessful implementation. The existing body of implementation literature (excluding the "show and tell" accounts) contains an impressive tilt toward implementation efforts that failed. We cannot be sure, however, if this represents sampling bias, measurement error, or an accurate picture of the track record in efforts to implement education innovations. Deficiencies in the definitions and measurement of successful implementation, as well as the short-term nature of most research, raise the probability that conclusions will portray a more dismal picture than perhaps is really the case.

Conclusions

The high mortality rate for educational innovations is more than simply a continuous search for better ways. Nor can abandonment of innovations be attributed entirely to local bureaucrats' attachment to the status quo. The federal government is a major funding source for school systems undertaking new programs. This chapter suggested that shifting federal priorities, preference for short-term results, and unpredictable funding discourage long-term commitments to implementation efforts. By continually staying on the hunt for new funds, school districts avoid the prospect of going from "feast to famine" following expiration of a lucrative federal grant. Some school districts are so successful that cadres of personnel spend their careers transferring from one to another "innovative" program.

However, such districts may be least successful, in the sense of implementing innovations, for they readily abandon programs as soon as external funds terminate. Prospects for implementation may be improved by linking grants to various kinds of local commitments—sometimes by matching funds (where this does not discriminate against the poorest districts), by agreements that tie the planning process to the school system's budget cycle, and, perhaps, by restricting initial funding to levels that school systems can realistically maintain on their own.

In the last analysis, however, policies of the funding agency can only affect the probability of implementing innovations if they modify the way in which school systems organize to deliver programs and services on a daily basis. I have argued that the research undertaken by social scientists, notably political scientists, has not contributed as much in this area as it might. Political scientists know far less about the nature of teacher interaction with clients than they do about political behavior of school board members and superintendents, and the major issues dealt with at the highest levels of authority. This has two immediate consequences. First, because political scientists focus primarily on school system leadership, they are better able to describe high level decision-making than to trace its impact on everyday classroom behavior. Second, viewing leaders as principal arbiters of conflict and as innovators often introduces subtle distortions into the findings. Urban school systems are typically portrayed as large bureaucracies with tight control exercised by the top decision-makers. A competing view —one that describes everyday teaching behavior in terms of the mismatch between expectations and resources, ambiguous roles, gaps between authority and responsibility—leads to quite different impressions. Discretion and autonomy are significant factors shaping teacher behavior. Much of the bias, impersonality, and rigidity attributed to bureaucracy appear exacerbated in schools where organizational procedures leave the most subjective and conflict-laden tasks to the personal judgment of individual teachers.

School bureaucracy is currently in the center of a political storm. There is no simple policy or administrative change that might remedy existing grievances or resolve current conflict. Based on the findings in this study, however, currently touted efforts to de-bureaucratize schools at the classroom level become increasingly suspect.

Appendix
Methodological Notes

Questionnaire Design

Several steps were necessary to translate the basic concepts of school bureaucracy and teacher attitudes into questionnaire items. First, general definitions of the basic terms and concepts were developed. For example, based upon prior research and teacher interviews, it was decided that, among the many aspects of bureaucracy, rules of behavior for the teacher have the most meaning for what goes on in the classroom on a daily basis and for the kind of relationships that evolve.

The second step was to identify specific items that would reflect the degree to which each of the basic concepts was present in the school or individual teacher. During this phase, several months were spent interviewing and observing teachers in the classroom to obtain information about specific behavioral and attitudinal items that have meaning for, and distinguish between, teachers. An initial questionnaire was written and pretested on a sample of teachers. It was then rewritten to eliminate or revise ambiguous questions and those with little variability among responses. It was again tested on a small group of teachers and found to be satisfactory.

Measurement

From responses to the final questionnaire, Guttman scales were developed to measure the basic dimensions of bureaucratization of teacher tasks and such teacher attitudes as hostility toward pupils, resistance to parental participation in school decision-making, resistance to innovation, routinization of classroom behavior, and hostility toward the principal. In constructing scales, items of apparent homogenous content were chosen. Questions with a response distribution greater than 80% to 20% were dropped.

The primary means of evaluating Guttman scales are the coefficients of reproducibility and scalability—both of which measure whether a scale meets the tests of unidimensionality and cumulativeness. By convention, acceptable cutoff points for the measures of reproducibility and scalability are .9 and .6, respectively. The scales used meet this standard.

Validity is defined as the extent to which items in a scale truly measure the intended attribute. There are several ways of testing validity; the most rigorous depend upon comparison with known independent measures of the intended attribute. Such outside measures are rarely available, particularly when the attribute is an artificial construct such as an attitude scale. In this study the concepts of "face" and "construct" validity were relied on. Face validity asserts that the items in a scale *seem* to measure what they purport to measure, although this is a matter of opinion. Readers may draw their own conclusions by reviewing the scales reprinted on the following pages.

Face validity can be supplemented by construct validity, which asserts a connection between the general definition of an attribute and the operational components of a scale by which it is gauged. In this study, for example, a general definition of the concept of bureaucracy is followed by a discussion of the empirical criteria used to measure school bureaucracy. It was decided that formal rules would offer the greatest prospect of objective, independent comparison among schools, and at the same time would delineate other bureaucratic characteristics such as hierarchy and impersonality, which are not directly measured. Hence, the scales of school bureaucracy focus on rules and procedures applicable to teachers in performing classroom tasks. Guttman scale scores for individual respondents were developed and averaged to obtain a measure of bureaucracy for each school as a whole. Each scale measures the extent to which particular teacher tasks are subject to formal school rules that are generally enforced.

A similar method was used to develop scales for teacher attitudes. Descriptive and analytic literature on teacher behavior, school organization, and school politics was reviewed. Aspects of teacher-client conflict were classified into various themes and interviews were conducted to identify specific items measuring several teacher attitudes. The questionnaire was designed, tested, and revised. From the final responses, Guttman scales were developed to measure six distinctive attitudes bearing on teacher performance.

The scales by which school bureaucracy and teacher attitudes were measured are printed on the following pages. In the interests of brevity, only scalable items are included, although the final questionnaire included standard questions about social and professional background, as well as items that proved to be non-scalable. The questionnaire items that follow also give an operational definition of each scale and the coding key used to classify responses; the actual questionnaire was arranged differently and contained neither definitions nor coding keys.* All responses were scored in dichotomous categories. Scale scores were ordered and also dichotomized, permitting use of Yule's Q as the primary test of association.

---

*Those interested in the actual questionnaire should see David Goodwin, "Teachers in the Public Schools: A Study of Organizational Structure, Social Class and Teacher Attitudes" (Ph.D. diss., The Johns Hopkins University, Baltimore, 1973).

Scales of School Bureaucracy

The following are the questionnaire items and coding that made up the scales by which the extent of school bureaucracy was measured.

Key	Coding
WR = Written Rule	WR and VR = 1
VR = Verbal Rule	NR and NE = 2
NR = No Rule	
NE = Rule Not Enforced	

Discipline Rules Scale (*)

In your school are there any rules or policies regarding:

1. How to handle discipline problems. WR ____ VR ____ NR ____ NE ____

2. Appropriate occasions to ask for assistance from the principal or vice-principal. WR ____ VR ____ NR ____ NE ____

3. Times during the day when children may not leave the classroom to go to the bathroom. WR ____ VR ____ NR ____ NE ____

4. How to handle fights between children. WR ____ VR ____ NR ____ NE ____

5. Putting children in the hall for discipline reasons. WR ____ VR ____ NR ____ NE ____

(*A system of rules and procedures dealing with typical work situations involving student discipline and order maintenance.)

Instruction Rules Scales (*)

In your school are there any rules or policies regarding:

1. Required preparation of lesson plans. WR ____ VR ____ NR ____ NE ____

2. Required approach for teaching
   mathematics.   WR ____ VR ____ NR ____ NE ____

3. Required approach for teaching
   reading.   WR ____ VR ____ NR ____ NE ____

4. The textbooks teachers must use.   WR ____ VR ____ NR ____ NE ____

(*A system of rules and procedures dealing with work situations involving student instruction.)

Parent-Teacher Communication Rules Scales (*)

1. Dress codes for teachers.   WR ___ VR ___ NR ___ NE ___

2. Use of standardized letter
   when writing to parents.   WR ___ VR ___ NR ___ NE ___

3. Appropriate times for parents
   to visit classes.   WR ___ VR ___ NR ___ NE ___

4. Criteria for not promoting
   children.   WR ___ VR ___ NR ___ NE ___

5. Visiting parents at home.   WR ___ VR ___ NR ___ NE ___

(*A system of rules and procedures dealing with typical work situations involving parent-teacher interaction.)

Scales for Teacher Attitudes

The following are the questionnaire items and coding that made up the scales by which teacher attitudes were measured.

Key	*Coding*
SA = Strongly Agree	SA and A = 1
A = Agree	D and SD = 2
D = Disagree	NS = 0
SD = Strongly Disagree	
NS = Not Sure	

Attitude Toward Parents (***)

1. Parents in this community don't appreciate the job teachers are doing. SA ___ A ___ D ___ SD ___ NS ___

2. A few parent groups can easily create problems in this school. SA ___ A ___ D ___ SD ___ NS ___

†3. Most parents in my school make a strong effort to teach their children respect for authority. SA ___ A ___ D ___ SD ___ NS ___

4. Parents in my school sometimes try to tell me how to do my job. SA ___ A ___ D ___ SD ___ NS ___

5. The presence of parents in the school can be a disrupting influence. SA ___ A ___ D ___ SD ___ NS ___

† For this item, coding is: SA and A = 2
D and SD = 1
NS = 0

(*Extent to which parents provide support for teacher authority.)

Custodial Orientation Toward Pupils (*)

1. Teaching in schools is getting
   to be a dangerous occupation.   SA ____ A ____ D ____ SD ____ NS ____

2. Students need more structure
   in school than they usually get
   at home.   SA ____ A ____ D ____ SD ____ NS ____

3. A teacher who is too friendly
   with the students is likely to
   lose his/her objectivity.   SA ____ A ____ D ____ SD ____ NS ____

4. Schools today are too permis-
   sive.   SA ____ A ____ D ____ SD ____ NS ____

5. The greatest problem in
   my school is ineffective
   discipline.   SA ____ A ____ D ____ SD ____ NS ____

(*Emphasis upon classroom discipline, teacher authority, and disorder; subordination of
pedagogical tasks.)

Attitude Toward the Principal (*)

1. The principal puts too many
   restrictions upon teachers in
   the classroom.   SA ____   A ____   D ____   SD ____   NS ____

2. The principal in my school is
   too concerned with his
   superior to consider
   the needs of teachers.   SA ____   A ____   D ____   SD ____   NS ____

†3. The principal in my school
   will usually accept ideas
   and suggestions from
   teachers.   SA ____   A ____   D ____   SD ____   NS ____

4. The principal in my school
   will often not back up the
   teacher in situations of
   conflict.   SA ____   A ____   D ____   SD ____   NS ____

†5. The principal in my school
   has the respect and confidence
   of the faculty.   SA ____   A ____   D ____   SD ____   NS ____

† For these items, coding is: SA and A = 2
                                 D and SD = 1
                                     NS = 0

(*Teacher perception of the extent to which principal exercises authority appropriately.)

Use of Routines in Classroom Management (*)

How frequently do you use each of the following classroom procedures and teaching techniques on a daily basis?

In my class children:

1. Receive permission before getting out of their seats.
   Always _____ Usually _____ Sometimes _____ Rarely _____ Never _____

2. Ask permission before going to the teacher's desk.
   Always _____ Usually _____ Sometimes _____ Rarely _____ Never _____

3. Sharpen pencils only at certain times of the day.
   Always _____ Usually _____ Sometimes _____ Rarely _____ Never _____

4. Go directly to their seats upon entering the room in the morning and hang up their clothing.
   Always _____ Usually _____ Sometimes _____ Rarely _____ Never _____

5. Stop all work when the class is noisy.
   Always _____ Usually _____ Sometimes _____ Rarely _____ Never _____

6. Do punishment homework if they misbehave.
   Always _____ Usually _____ Sometimes _____ Rarely _____ Never _____

Coding for Items 1, 2, and 6
Always and Usually = 1
Sometimes, Rarely, and Never = 2

Coding for Items 3, 4, and 5
Always, usually and sometimes = 1
Rarely and never = 2

(*A common device to regularize classroom behavior.)

Attitude Toward Parental Participation (*)

Please circle the one alternative which most approximates your opinion of the proper role parents should have in areas of school policy. The alternatives are:

Key
1 = Total Control
2 = Shared Control with Administrators
    and Teachers
3 = A Chance to Voice an Opinion
4 = Not an Appropriate Role for Parents

1. Spending school funds.	1	2	3	4
2. Disciplining students.	1	2	3	4
3. Adopting new programs such as sex education.	1	2	3	4
4. Curriculum changes such as modern math, foreign language, etc.	1	2	3	4
5. General school policies.	1	2	3	4

Coding
1 and 2 = 1
3 and 4 = 2

(*Receptivity toward parental participation in school decision-making.)

Attitude Toward School Innovation (*)

Please select one alternative (yes, no, undecided) which comes closest to your opinion.

1. Are you in favor of using
   teaching machines for instruc-
   tional purposes?   Yes ____ No ____ Undecided ____

2. Are you in favor of requiring
   experienced teachers to teach
   in inner-city schools for a
   certain number of years?   Yes ____ No ____ Undecided ____

3. Do you favor the decentralization
   of schools in Baltimore?   Yes ____ No ____ Undecided ____

4. Would you like to have a parent aide
   in the classroom?   Yes ____ No ____ Undecided ____

          Coding
             Yes = 1
    Undecided and No = 2

(*A general receptivity to educational change.)

Notes

Chapter 1

1. Michael Lipsky, "Toward A Theory of Street Level Bureaucracy" (paper presented at annual meeting of American Political Science Association, 1969).
2. Woodrow Wilson, "The Study of Administration," *Political Science Quarterly*, vol. ii (June 1887), p. 212.
3. Francis E. Rourke, *Bureaucracy, Politics, and Public Policy* (Boston: Little, Brown & Co., 1969), p. 51.
4. Raymond Rist. *The Urban School: A Factory for Failure* (Cambridge: M.I.T. Press, 1973), pp. 241-42.
5. James Coleman et al., *Equality of Educational Opportunity* (Washington, D.C.: U.S. Government Printing Office, 1966), pp. 3-34.
6. David Rogers, *110 Livingston Street* (New York: Vintage Books, 1969), p. 267.
7. Floyd Hunter, *Community Power Structure: A Study of Decision-Makers* (Chapel Hill: University of North Carolina Press, 1953); and C. Wright Mills, *The Power Elite* (New York: Oxford University Press, 1956).
8. Nelson Polsby, *Community Power and Political Theory* (New Haven: Yale University Press, 1963), pp. 45-68.
9. Robert Dahl, *Who Governs?* (New Haven: Yale University Press, 1961), pp. 141-62.

10. Wallace Sayre and Herbert Kaufman, *Governing New York City* (New York: Russell Sage Foundation, 1960), p. 285.
11. Theodore Lowi, "Machine Politics—Old and New," *Public Interest*, no. 9 (Fall 1967), pp. 83-92.
12. Robert Crain, *The Politics of School Desegregation* (Garden City, N.Y.: Doubleday & Co., 1969), p. 378.
13. Rogers, *110 Livingston St.*, p. 584.
14. Marilyn Gittell, "Professionalism and Public Participation in Educational Policy-Making: New York City, A Case Study," in Marilyn Gittell and Alan Hevesi, eds., *The Politics of Urban Education* (New York: Praeger Publishers, 1969), p. 175.
15. James Q. Wilson, *Varieties of Police Behavior* (Cambridge: Harvard University Press, 1968), p. 7.
16. Charles Bidwell, "The School as a Formal Organization," in James March, ed., *Handbook of Organizations* (Chicago: Rand McNally, 1965), pp. 975-77.
17. C. Wayne Gordon, "The Role of the Teacher in the Social Structure of the High School," *Journal of Educational Sociology*, vol. 29, no. 1 (September 1955), pp. 21-29.
18. Lipsky, "Theory of Street Level Bureaucracy."
19. Harold Hodgkinson (address at National Institute of Education, Education and Work Forum, Shoreham Hotel, Washington, D.C., February 9, 1976).
20. Kenneth Dolbeare and Phillip Hammond, *The School Prayer Decisions: From Court Policy to Local Practice* (Chicago: University of Chicago Press, 1971).
21. J.T. Goodlad and M.E. Klein, *Behind the Classroom Door* (New York: Charles A. Jones Publishing Co., 1970); see also, Neal Gross, Joseph Giacquinta, and Marilyn Bernstein, *Implementing Organizational Innovations: A Sociological Analysis of Planned Educational Change* (New York: Basic Books, 1971).
22. See Rist, *The Urban School*, p. 19; see also, Robert Rosenthal and Lenore Jacobson, *Pygmalion in the Classroom* (New York: Holt, Rinehart & Winston, 1968).
23. Robert Herriott and Nancy Hoyt St. John, *Social Class and the Urban School* (New York: John Wiley & Sons, 1966), pp. 83-108.
24. Lipsky, "Theory of Street Level Bureaucracy," p. 1.
25. Peter Rossi et al., "Between Black and White: The Faces of American Institutions in the Ghetto," *Supplemental Studies for the National Advisory Commission on Civil Disorders* (New York: Praeger Publishers, 1968), p. 74.
26. Herriott and St. John, *Social Class and the Urban School*, pp. 7-8.
27. David Ryan, *Characteristics of Teachers* (Washington, D.C.: American Council on Education, 1960), pp. 390-91.
28. W.W. Charters, Jr., "The Social Background of Teaching," in N.L. Gage, ed., *Handbook of Research on Teaching* (Chicago: Rand McNally, 1963), p. 726.
29. Robert Merton, "Bureaucratic Structure and Personality," in Robert Merton et al., eds., *Reader in Bureaucracy* (Glencoe, Ill.: Free Press, 1952), pp. 365-66.

30. James Anderson, *Bureaucracy in Education* (Baltimore: Johns Hopkins University Press, 1968), pp. 18, 170-71.
31. Jerome Skolnick, *Justice Without Trial* (New York: John Wiley & Sons, 1966), pp. 3-9.
32. Wilson, *Varieties of Police Behavior*, pp. 16-56.
33. Bryan Wilson, "The Teacher's Role—A Sociological Analysis," *British Journal of Sociology*, vol. 13, no. 1 (March 1962), pp. 15-32; and Amitai Etzioni, ed., *The Semi-Professions and Their Organizations* (New York: Free Press, 1969), pp. v-xvi.
34. Martin Deutsch, "Minority Group and Class Status as Related to Social and Personality Factors in Scholastic Achievement," Society For Applied Anthropology, Ithaca, New York (Monograph no. 2, 1960), p. 23.
35. Joy Haralick, "Teacher Acceptance of Administrative Action," *Journal of Experimental Education*, vol. 37, no. 2 (Winter 1968), p. 44.
36. Coleman, *Equality of Educational Opportunity*, pp. 737.
37. For examples, see Peter Blau and Otis Dudley Duncan, *American Occupational Structure* (New York: John Wiley & Sons, 1967); Karl Alexander and Bruce Eckland, *The Effect of Education on the Social Mobility of High School Sophomores Fifteen Years Later (1955-1970)*, Institute for Research on Poverty, University of North Carolina, November 1973; Christopher Jencks et al., *Inequality: A Reassessment of the Effect of Family and Schooling in America* (New York: Basic Books, 1972); William Sewell et al., "The Educational and Early Occupational Attainment Process: Replication and Revision," *American Sociological Review*, vol. 35, no. 6 (December 1970), pp. 1014-27; Colin Greer, *The Great School Legend* (New York: Basic Books, 1972); and Ivan Illich, *De-Schooling Society* (Garden City, N.Y.: Doubleday & Co., 1971).
38. Based on an economic survey conducted by the Baltimore City Public Schools, Division of Research and Development, May 1970.
39. Baltimore City Public Schools, *Annual Report of Student Body Racial Composition*, September 1970.
40. H.H. Gerth and C. Wright Mills, eds., *From Max Weber: Essays In Sociology* (New York: Oxford University Press, 1958), pp. 196-98, 214.
41. Richard Hall, "An Empirical Study of Bureaucratic Dimensions and Their Relation to Other Organizational Characteristics" (Ph.D. diss., Ohio State University, 1961); and David McKay, "An Empirical Study of Bureaucratic Dimensions and Their Relation to Other Characteristics of School Organization" (Ph.D. diss., University of Alberta, Edmonton, 1964).
42. Keith Punch, "Bureaucratic Structure in Schools: Toward Redefinition and Measurement," *Educational Administration Quarterly*, vol. 5, no. 2 (Spring 1969), p. 50; and Stanley Udy, Jr., "Bureaucracy and Rationality in Weber's Organization Theory: An Empirical Study," *American Sociological Review*, vol. 24, no. 6 (December 1959), pp. 791-95. Udy has argued that those aspects of bureaucracy that emphasize "rationality"—expertise, limited objectives, and technical competence—are negatively associated with other bureaucratic dimensions such as hierarchy, authority, rules, and procedures. The decision in

the present study to focus on one aspect of bureaucracy—formal rules—is justified because much of the anti-bureaucratic literature emphasizes rules and procedures as the prime determinants of "pathological" behavior.

43. Merton, *Reader in Bureaucracy*, p. 361-71.
44. Howard Becker, "Teacher in the Authority Structure of the Public School," *Journal of Educational Sociology*, vol. 27 (November 1953), pp. 135-36; Gordon, "Role of the Teacher," pp. 22-24; and Haralick, "Teacher Acceptance of Administrative Action," pp. 39-47.
45. Gordon, "Role of the Teacher," p. 23.
46 Anderson, "Bureaucracy in Education," pp. 170-71.
47. Norman Robinson, "A Study of the Bureaucratic Role Orientations of Teachers and Principal and Their Relationship to Bureaucratic Characteristics of School Organization" (Ph.D. diss., University of Alberta, Edmonton, 1966), p. 204.

Chapter II

1. Coleman et al., *Equality of Educational Opportunity*, pp. 3-34.
2. Howard Becker, "The Career of the Chicago Public School Teacher," *American Journal of Sociology*, vol. 57, no. 5 (March 1952), p. 470.
3. Baltimore City Public Schools, Division of Research and Development, *Annual Report of Student Body Racial Composition*, September 1970.
4. Daniel Patrick Moynihan, *The Negro Family: The Case for National Action* (Washington, D.C.: U.S. Department of Labor), March 1965.
5. Herriott and St. John, *Social Class and the Urban School*, p. 97.
6. Ibid., pp. 57-62.
7. Ibid., pp. 57-79.
8. Eric Hanushek, *The Value of Teachers In Teaching* (Santa Monica: Rand Corporation, December 1970), pp. 14-19.
9. Samuel Bowles, "Toward Equality of Educational Opportunity," in *Harvard Educational Review*, ed., *Equal Educational Opportunity* (Cambridge: Harvard University Press, 1969), pp. 120-21.
10. Herriott and St. John, *Social Class and the Urban School*, pp. 83-108.
11. Anderson, *Bureaucracy in Education*, pp. 148-49.
12. Rossi, "Between Black and White," p. 74.
13. William G. Spady, "The Authority System of the School and Student Unrest: A Theoretical Exploration," in C. Wayne Gordon, ed., *Uses of the Sociology of Education*, 73rd Yearbook of the National Society for Study of Education (Chicago: University of Chicago Press, 1974), p. 38.
14. Michael Lipsky, "Street Level Bureaucracy and Urban Reform," in Virginia Ermer and John Strange, eds., *Blacks and the Bureaucracy* (New York: Thomas Crowell, 1972), pp. 171-73.
15. Seymour Sarason, *The Culture of the School and the Problem of Change* (Boston: Allyn & Bacon, 1971), pp. 62-87.
16. Herriott and St. John, *Social Class and the Urban School*, pp. 42-43; and M.

Kent Jennings, "Parental Grievances and School Politics," *Public Opinion Quarterly*, vol. 32 (Fall 1968), p. 377.

17. Hess and Shipman, cited in Robert Strom, ed., *The Inner City Classroom: Teacher Behaviors*, (Columbus: Charles Merrill, 1968), p. 16; and Sam Sieber and David Wilder, "Teaching Styles: Parental Preferences and Professional Role Definitions," *Sociology of Education*, vol. 40 (1967), p. 310.

Chapter III

1. Michel Crozier, *The Bureaucratic Phenomenon* (Chicago: University of Chicago Press, 1964), p. 3.
2. Gerth and Mills, *From Max Weber*, pp. 196-244.
3. Merton, *Reader in Bureaucracy*, pp. 365-66.
4. Amitai Etzioni, *A Comparative Analysis of Complex Organizations* (New York: Free Press, 1961), pp. 3-39.
5. Spady, "Authority System of the School," p. 9.
6. Gerth and Mills, *From Max Weber*, pp. 196-244.
7. Ibid., pp. 196-244; and Herbert Simon, *Administrative Behavior* (New York: MacMillan & Co., 1947), pp. 11-16.
8. Hall, "Study of Bureaucratic Dimensions," pp. 36-37.
9. Gerth and Mills, *From Max Weber*, p. 211.
10. Stanley H. Udy, Jr., "The Comparative Analysis of Organizations," in James March, ed., *Handbook of Organizations* (Chicago: Rand McNally, 1965), p. 693.
11. Alvin Gouldner, "Metaphysical Pathos and the Theory of Bureaucracy," in Amitai Etzioni, ed., *A Sociological Reader on Complex Organizations* (New York: Holt, Rinehart & Winston, 1961), p. 74; and Peter Blau, *Bureaucracy in Modern Society* (New York: Random House, 1956), p. 20.
12. McKay, "An Empirical Study," pp. 86-87.
13. Anderson, *Bureaucracy in Education*, p. 85.
14. Raymond Adams, Richard Kimble, Marjorie Marlin, "School Size, Organizational Structure, and Teacher Practices," *Educational Administration Quarterly*, vol. 16, no. 3 (Autumn 1970), p. 15; Hall, "Bureaucratic Dimensions," p. 40; and Robinson, "Bureaucratic Role Orientations," p. 137.
15. Richard Hall, Eugene Haas, Norman Jacobson, "Organizational Size, Complexity and Formalization," *American Sociological Review*, vol. 32 (December 1967), p. 911.
16. Alvin Gouldner, "The Problem of Succession in Bureaucracy," in Merton, *Reader in Bureaucracy*, p. 349.
17. Udy, "Comparative Analysis of Organizations," p. 693.
18. Anderson, *Bureaucracy in Education*, p. 102.
19. Keith Punch, "Bureaucratic Structure in Schools and Its Relationship to Leadership Behavior: An Empirical Study" (Ph.D. diss., University of Toronto, 1967), p. 158.
20. Stanley H. Udy, Jr., *Organization of Work: A Comparative Analysis of Pro-*

duction Among Non-Industrial Peoples (New Haven: HRAF Press, 1959), p. 38.

21. Eugene Litwak, "Models of Bureaucracy Which Permit Conflict," *American Journal of Sociology*, vol. 67, no. 2 (September 1961), p. 177.
22. Gerald Popiel, "Bureaucracy in the Mass Industrial Union," *Journal of Economics and Sociology*, vol. 15, no. 1 (October 1955), pp. 49-55.
23. Hall, "Bureaucratic Dimensions," pp. 42, 46.
24. Anderson, *Bureaucracy in Education*, p. 95.
25. Ibid., pp. 169-173; Amitai Etzioni, *Modern Organizations* (Englewood Cliffs: Prentice-Hall, 1964), pp. 75-93; Robert Peabody, "Perceptions of Organizational Authority: A Comparative Analysis," *Administrative Science Quarterly*, vol. 6, no. 4 (March 1962), pp. 423-25; and Victor Thompson, *Modern Organization* (New York: Alfred A. Knopf, 1961).
26. Robinson, "Bureaucratic Role Orientations," p. 34.
27. Ibid., p. 137.
28. Anderson, *Bureaucracy in Education*, pp. 97, 100.
29. Steven Arthur Waldhorn, "Pathological Bureaucracies," in Ermer and Strange, *Blacks and the Bureaucracy*, pp. 184-91; and Orion White, "Dialectical Organization: An Alternative to Bureaucracy," *Public Administration Review*, vol. 29, no. 1 (January/February 1969), pp. 32-40.
30. Anderson, *Bureaucracy in Education*, p. 86.
31. White, "Dialectical Organization," pp. 32-40.
32. Anderson, *Bureaucracy in Education*, p. 85.
33. Alvin Gouldner, *Patterns of Industrial Bureaucracy* (Glencoe, Ill.: Free Press, 1954), p. 63.
34. Becker, "Teacher in the Authority Structure," p. 134, and Haralick, Teacher Acceptance of Administrative Behavior," p. 44.
35. Peter Blau and W. Richard Scott, *Formal Organizations* (San Francisco: Chandler, 1962), p. 113.
36. Anderson, *Bureaucracy in Education*, p. 102.

Chapter IV

1. Gerth and Mills, *From Max Weber*, p. 215.
2. Simon, *Administrative Behavior*, p. 408.
3. Blau and Scott, *Formal Organizations*, pp. 87-99.
4. Merton, "Bureaucratic Structure and Personality," pp. 361-71.
5. Gouldner, *Patterns of Industrial Bureaucracy*, pp. 93-100.
6. Crozier, *The Bureaucratic Phenomenon*, p. 207.
7. Charles Bonjean and Michael Grimes, "Bureaucracy and Alienation: A Dimensional Approach," *Social Forces*, vol. 48, no. 3 (March 1970), p. 371.
8. Melvin Kohn, "Bureaucratic Man: A Portrait and an Interpretation," *American Sociological Review*, vol. 36 (June 1971), p. 465.
9. Anderson, *Bureaucracy in Education*, pp. 127, 135.
10. Gerald Moeller and W.W. Charters, "Relation of Bureaucratization to the

Sense of Power Among Teachers," *Administrative Science Quarterly*, vol. 10, no. 4 (March 1966), p. 457.

11. Elihu Katz and S.N. Eisenstadt, "Some Sociological Observations on the Response of Israeli Organizations to New Immigrants," *Administrative Science Quarterly*, vol. 5 (June 1960), pp. 113-33.
12. Becker, "Teacher in the Authority Structure," p. 130; also Haralick, Teacher Acceptance of Administrative Action," p. 44.
13. The Gallup Poll indicates that public attitudes toward schools are quite favorable regarding the level of teaching competence and instructional ability of teachers. However, there is a general sense that schools have failed in handling student discipline problems. See George Gallup, "Fourth Annual Gallup Poll of Public Attitudes Toward Education," *Phi Delta Kappan* (September 1972), p. 34.
14. Wilson, *Varieties of Police Behavior*, pp. 16-56.
15. William Rosengren, "Communication, Organization and Conduct in the Therapeutic Milieu," *Administrative Science Quarterly*, vol. 9, no. 1 (June 1964), pp. 69-90.
16. Daniel Katz and Robert Kahn, *The Social Psychology of Organizations* (New York: John Wiley & Sons, 1966), p. 49.
17. Ralph Ruddock, *Roles and Relationships* (London: Routledge and Kegan Paul, 1969), p. 33.
18. Becker, "Teacher in the Authority Structure," pp. 129-39.
19. Paul Bowman and Charles Matthews, cited in Strom, *Inner City Classroom*, p. 83.
20. Jennings, "Parental Grievances," pp. 365-66.
21. Becker, "Teacher in the Authority Structure," p. 130; and Sieber, "Teaching Styles," p. 310.
22. Bruce Biddle, Howard Rosencranz, and Earl Rankin, "Studies in the Role of the Public School Teacher," Social Psychology Laboratory, University of Missouri, Columbia, vol. 2, June 1961, pp. 150-51.
23. Hess and Shipman, in Strom, *Inner City Classroom*, pp. 15-16.
24. Paul Hant and Elvin Rasof, "Discipline: Function or Task," in Strom, *Inner City Classroom*, p. 167.
25. Sieber, "Teaching Styles," p. 310.
26. Gordon, "Role of the Teacher," p. 25.
27. Robinson, "Bureaucratic Role Orientations," p. 204.
28. Becker, "Teacher in the Authority Structure," pp. 133-39.

Chapter V

1. See the arguments summarized in George R. La Noue and Bruce L.R. Smith, *The Politics of School Decentralization* (Lexington, Mass.: D.C. Heath & Co., 1973), pp. 1-23.
2. Charters, "The Social Background of Teaching," p. 726.
3. Anderson, *Bureaucracy in Education*, pp. 144-45.

4. Egon Guba, Philip Jackson, and Charles Bidwell, "Occupational Choice and the Teaching Career," *Educational Research Bulletin*, vol. 38, no. 1 (January 1959), pp. 10-11.
5. Harmon Ziegler, *The Political Life of American Teachers* (Englewood Cliffs: Prentice-Hall, 1967).
6. Louis Smith and William Geoffrey, *Complexities of an Urban Classroom* (New York: Holt, Rinehart & Winston, 1968), pp. 25-30; Gordon, "The Role of the Teacher," pp. 21-29; and Willard Waller, *Sociology of Teaching* (New York: John Wiley & Sons, 1932), p. 1.
7. Rosenthal and Jacobson, *Pygmalion in the Classroom;* and Strom, *Inner City Classroom*, pp. 44-56, 93-110.
   44-56, 93-110.
8. Anderson, *Bureaucracy in Education*, pp. 144-45.

Chapter VI

1. Charles Silberman, *Crisis in the Classroom: The Remaking of American Education* (New York: Random House, 1970), p. 9.
2. Robert Dreeben, *On What Is Learned in School* (Reading, Mass.: Addison-Wesley, 1968).
3. Waller, *Sociology of Teaching*, pp. 386-400; Ziegler, *American Teachers;* and Marilyn Gittell and T. Edward Hollander, *Six Urban School Districts: A Comparative Study of Institutional Response* (New York: Praeger Publishers, 1968).
4. Ronald and Mary Havelock, "Educational Innovation in the United States: The National Survey," National Institute of Education, OEG-0-70-4296 (508), May 1973, p. 15.
5. Gordon Cawelti, "Innovative Practices in High Schools," *Nation's Schools*, LXXIX (April 1967), pp. 64-66. For case studies on the abandonment of innovations, see Louis Smith and Patricia Keith, *Anatomy of Educational Innovation* (New York: John Wiley & Sons, 1971); and Neal Gross, Marilyn Bernstein, and Joseph Giacquinta, *Implementing Organizational Innovations: A Sociological Analysis of Planned Educational Change* (New York: Basic Books, 1971).
6. Jon Goodlad, Frances Klein, and Associates, *Behind the Classroom Door* (Worthington, Ohio: Charles Jones, 1970), pp. 72-73.
7. Carol Van Deusen Lukas, "Problems of Implementing Head Start Planned Variation Models," in Alice Rivlin and P. Michael Timpane, eds., *Planned Variation in Education* (Washington, D.C.: Brookings Institution, 1975), pp. 113-25.
8. Ronald Havelock, "Planning for Innovation Through Dissemination and Utilization of Knowledge," Center for Research on the Utilization of Scientific Knowledge, University of Michigan (U.S. Office of Education grant, 1969), Chapters 10-11.
9. John Pincus, "Incentives for Innovation in the Public Schools," *Review of*

Educational Research, vol. 44, no. 1 (Winter 1974), p. 114.

10. *Washington Post,* December 17, 1974, p. C1.

11. Graham Allison, *Essence of Decision: Explaining the Cuban Missile Crisis* (Boston: Little, Brown & Co., 1971); and David Halberstam, *The Best and the Brightest* (New York: Random House, 1973).

12. Herbert Simon, *Models of Man* (New York: John Wiley & Sons, 1957), p. 198.

13. John De Arman, "The Abandonment Rate and Causes of Abandonment of Innovations in Secondary Schools" (National Institute of Education, G-74-0005, unpublished preliminary data).

14. P. Berman and M.W. McLaughlin, "Implementing Innovations: Revisions for an Agenda for a Study of Change Agent Programs in Education," Rand Corporation, Santa Monica, California, WN-8450-1-HWW, November 1973, p. 15.

15. Crain, *Politics of School Desegregation,* pp. 111-14, 135-36.

16. Berman and McLaughlin, "Implementing Innovations," p. 13.

17. David Selznick, *TVA and the Grass Roots* (Berkeley and Los Angeles: University of California Press, 1949).

18. Crozier, *Bureaucratic Phenomenon,* p. 199.

19. For a review of this literature, see Michael Fullan and Alan Pomfret, "Critical Review of Research on Curriculum Implementation" (National Institute of Education 74-0122, August 1974, unpublished draft).

Selected
Bibliography

Books

Anderson, James. *Bureaucracy in Education*. Baltimore: Johns Hopkins University Press, 1968.

Allison, Graham T. *The Essence of Decision: Explaining The Cuban Missile Crisis*. Boston: Little, Brown & Co., 1971.

Biddle, Bruce; Rosencranz, Howard; and Rankin, Earl. *Studies in the Role of the Public School Teacher*. vol. 2. Social Psychology Laboratory, University of Missouri, Columbia, 1961.

Blau, Peter. *Dynamics of Bureaucracy*. Chicago: University of Chicago Press, 1955.

Blau, Peter, and Scott, W. Richard. *Formal Organizations*. San Francisco: Chandler Press, 1962.

Crain, Robert. *The Politics of School Desegregation*. Garden City, N. Y.: Doubleday & Co., 1969.

Crozier, Michel. *Bureaucratic Phenomenon*. Chicago: University of Chicago Press, 1964.

Dahl, Robert. *Who Governs?* New Haven: Yale University Press, 1961.

Dolbeare, Kenneth, and Hammond, P.M. *School Prayer Decisions: From Court Policy to Local Practice*. Chicago: University of Chicago Press, 1971.

Dornbusch, Sanford, and Scott, W. Richard. *Evaluation and the Exercise of Authority*. San Francisco: Jossey-Bass Publishers, 1975.

Dreeben, Robert. *On What is Learned in School*. Reading, Mass.: Addison-Wesley Co., 1968.

Edelman, Jacob Murray. *The Symbolic Uses of Politics*. Urbana: University of Illinois Press, 1964.

Edwards, Allan. *Techniques of Attitude Scale Construction*. New York: Appleton-Century-Crofts, 1957.

Ermer, Virginia, and Strange, John, eds. *Blacks and the Bureaucracy*. New York: Thomas Crowell, 1972.

Etzioni, Amitai. *A Comparative Analysis of Complex Organizations*. New York: Free Press, 1961.

Etzioni, Amitai. *Modern Organizations*. Englewood Cliffs: Prentice-Hall, 1964.

Etzioni, Amitai, ed. *The Semi-Professions and Their Organizations*. New York: Free Press, 1969.

Etzioni, Amitai, ed. *A Sociological Reader on Complex Organizations*. New York: Random House, 1956.

Festinger, Leon. *A Theory of Cognitive Dissonance*. Evanston, Ill.: Row and Peterson, 1957.

Gerth, H.H., and Mills, C. Wright. *From Max Weber: Essays in Sociology*. New York: Oxford University Press, 1958.

Goodlad, John; Klein, M. Frances; and Associates. *Behind the Classroom Door*. Worthington, Ohio: C.A. Jones Publishing Co., 1970.

Gouldner, Alvin, *Patterns of Industrial Bureaucracy*. Glencoe, Ill.: Free Press, 1954.

Gross, Neal; Giacquinta, Joseph B.; and Bernstein, Marilyn. *Implementing Organizational Innovations: A Sociological Analysis of Planned Educational Change*. New York: Basic Books, 1971.

Hage, Jerald, and Aiken, Michael. *Sociological Change in Complex Organizations*. New York: Random House, 1970.

Herriott, Robert, and St. John, Nancy Hoyt. *Social Class and the Urban School*. New York: John Wiley & Sons, 1966.

Hunter, Floyd. *Community Power Structure: A Study of Decision-Makers*. Chapel Hill: University of North Carolina Press, 1953.

Jackson, Philip. *Life in the Classroom*. New York: Holt, Rinehart and Winston, 1968.

Kahn, Robert; Wolfe, Donald; Quinn, Robert; and Snoek, J. Diedrick. *Organizational Stress: Studies in Role Conflict and Ambiguity*. New York: John Wiley & Sons, 1964.

Katz, Daniel, and Kahn, Robert. *The Social Psychology of Organizations*. New York: John Wiley & Sons, 1966.

Kaufman, Herbert. *The Forest Ranger*. Baltimore: Johns Hopkins University Press, 1960.

Kaufman, Herbert. *Limits of Organizational Change*. University, Ala.: University of Alabama Press, 1971.

LaNoue, George R., and Smith, Bruce L. R. *The Politics of School Decentralization*. Lexington, Mass.: Lexington Books, 1973.

Leacock, Eleanor. *Teaching and Learning in City Schools*. New York: Basic Books, 1969.

Levy, Frank; Meltsner, Arnold J.; and Wildavsky, Aaron. *Urban Outcomes: Streets, Schools and Libraries*. Berkeley: University of California Press, 1974.

Lortie, Daniel C. *Schoolteacher; A Sociological Study*. Chicago: University of Chicago Press, 1975.

Mann, Dale. *Policy Decision-Making in Education*. New York: Teachers College Press, 1975.

Mills, C. Wright. *The Power Elite*. New York: Oxford University Press, 1956.

Moore, Wilbert. *The Professions: Roles and Rules*. New York: Russell Sage Foundation, 1970.

Oppenheim, A.N. *Questionnaire Design and Attitude Measurement*. New York: Basic Books, 1966.

Polsby, Nelson. *Community Power and Political Theory*. New Haven: Yale University Press, 1963.

Pressman, Jeffrey, and Wildavsky, Aaron. *Implementation*. Berkeley: University of California Press, 1973.

Rivlin, Alice M., and Timpane, P. Michael, eds. *Planned Variation in Education*. Washington, D.C.: Brookings Institution, 1975.

Rogers, David. *110 Livingston Street*. New York: Random House, 1969.

Rourke, Francis. *Bureaucracy, Politics and Public Policy*. Boston: Little, Brown & Co., 1969.

Ruddock, Ralph. *Roles and Relationships*. London: Routledge & Kegan Paul, 1969.

Ryans, David. *Characteristics of Teachers*. Washington, D.C.: American Council on Education, 1960.

Sarason, Seymour B. *The Culture of the School and the Problem of Change*. Boston: Allyn & Bacon, 1971.

Sayre, Wallace, and Kaufman, Herbert. *Governing New York City*. New York: Russell Sage Foundation, 1960.

Selznick, David. *TVA and the Grass Roots*. Berkeley: University of California Press, 1949.

Sexton, Patricia C. *Education and Income*. New York: Viking Press, 1961.

Silberman, Charles. *Crisis in the Classroom: The Remaking of American Education*. New York: Random House, 1970.

Simon, Herbert. *Administrative Behavior*. New York: MacMillan, 1947.

Skolnick, Jerome. *Justice Without Trial*. New York: John Wiley & Sons, 1966.

Smith, Louis, and Geoffrey, William. *Complexities of the Urban Classroom*. New York: Holt, Rinehart & Winston, 1968.

Smith, Louis, and Keith, Patricia. *Anatomy of an Educational Innovation*. New York: John Wiley & Sons, 1971.

Stouffer, Samuel; and others. *Measurement and Prediction*. New York: John Wiley & Sons, 1950.

Strom, Robert, ed. *The Inner City Classroom: Teacher Behaviors.* Columbus: Charles Merrill, 1968.

Thompson, Victor. *Modern Organization.* New York: Alfred Knopf, 1961.

Torgerson, Warren. *Theory and Method of Scaling.* New York: John Wiley & Sons, 1967.

Waller, Willard. *Sociology of Teaching.* New York: John Wiley & Sons, 1932.

Wilson, James Q. *Varieties of Police Behavior.* Cambridge: Harvard University Press, 1968.

Ziegler, Harmon. *Political Life of American Teachers.* Englewood Cliffs: Prentice-Hall, 1967.

Articles and Monographs

Becker, Howard. "The Career of the Chicago Public School Teacher." *American Journal of Sociology* 57(1952):470-477.

Becker, Howard. "Social Class Variations in the Teacher-Pupil Relationship." *Journal of Educational Sociology* 25(1952):451-465.

Becker, Howard. "Teacher in the Authority Structure of the Public School." *Journal of Educational Sociology* 27(1953):128-141.

Bidwell, Charles. "The School as a Formal Organization." In *Handbook of Organizations*, edited by James March, pp. 972-1022. Chicago: Rand McNally, 1965.

Bonjean, Charles, and Grimes, Michael. "Bureaucracy and Alienation: A Dimensional Approach." *Social Forces* 48(1970):365-373.

Charters, W.W., Jr. "The Social Background of Teaching." In *Handbook of Research on Teaching*, edited by N.L. Gage, pp. 715-783. Chicago: Rand McNally, 1963.

Clark, Burton. "Organizational Adaptation and Precarious Values." *American Sociological Review* 21(1956):327-336.

Gittell, Marilyn. "Professionalism and Public Participation in Educational Policy-Making: New York City, A Case Study." In *The Politics of Urban Education*, edited by Marilyn Gittell, Alan Hevesi, pp. 155-177. New York: Praeger Publishers, 1969.

Gordon, C. Wayne. "The Role of the Teacher in the Social Structure of the High School." *Journal of Educational Sociology* 29(1955):21-29.

Guba, Egon, and Bidwell, Charles. *Administrative Relationships: Teacher Effectiveness, Teacher Satisfaction, and Administrative Behavior.* Chicago: Midwest Administration Center, University of Chicago, 1957.

Guba, Egon; Jackson, Philip; and Bidwell, Charles. "Occupational Choice and the Teaching Career." *Educational Research Bulletin* 38(1959).

Hall, Richard; Haas, Eugene; and Jacobson, Norman. "Organizational Size, Complexity, and Formalization." *American Sociological Review* 32(1967):904-912.

Hanushek, Eric. *The Value of Teachers in Teaching.* Santa Monica: Rand Corporation, 1970.

Haralick, Joy Gold. "Teacher Acceptance of Administrative Action." *Journal of Experimental Education* 37(1968):37-47.

Jennings, M. Kent. "Parental Grievances and School Politics." *Public Opinion Quarterly* 32(1968):363-378.

Katz, Elihu, and Eisenstadt, S.N. "Some Sociological Observations On the Response of Israeli Organizations to New Immigrants." *Administrative Science Quarterly* 5(1960):113-133.

Kohn, Melvin. "Bureaucratic Man: A Portrait and an Interpretation." *American Sociological Review* 36(1971):461-474.

Lindblom, Charles. "Science of Muddling Through." *Public Administration Review* 19(1959):79-88.

Lipsky, Michael. "Toward A Theory of Street Level Bureaucracy." American Political Science Association, 1969.

Litwak, Eugene. "Models of Bureaucracy Which Permit Conflict." *American Journal of Sociology* 67(1961):177-184.

Lowi, Theodore. "Machine Politics—Old and New." *Public Interest* 9(1967):83-92.

Mason, Ward; Dressel, Robert; and Bain, Robert. "Sex Role and Career Orientations of Beginning Teachers." *Harvard Educational Review* 29(1959):370-383.

Merton, Robert. "Bureaucratic Structure and Personality." In *Reader in Bureaucracy*, edited by Robert Merton et al., pp. 361-371. Glencoe, Ill.: Free Press, 1952.

Moeller, Gerald, and Charters, W.W. "Relation of Bureaucratization to the Sense of Power Among Teachers." *Administrative Science Quarterly* 10(1966):444-465.

Peabody, Robert. "Perceptions of Organizational Authority: A Comparative Analysis." *Administrative Science Quarterly* 6(1962):463-482.

Peabody, Robert, and Rourke, Francis, "Public Bureaucracies," In *Handbook of Organizations*, edited by James March, pp. 802-837. Chicago: Rand McNally, 1965.

Pincus, John. "Incentives for Innovation in Public Schools." *Review of Educational Research* 44(1974):113-144.

Pugh, D.S.; Hickson, D.J.; and Hinings, C.R. "An Empirical Taxonomy of Work Organizations." *Administrative Science Quarterly* 14(1969):115-126.

Punch, Keith. "Bureaucratic Structure in Schools: Toward Redefinition and Measurement." *Educational Administration Quarterly* 5(1969):43-57.

Rosengren, William. "Communication, Organization and Conflict in the 'Therapeutic Milieu'." *Administrative Science Quarterly* 9(1964):69-90.

Sieber, Sam, and Wilder, David. "Teaching Styles: Parental Preferences and Professional Role Definitions." *Sociology of Education* 40(1967):302-315.

Spady, William G. "The Authority System of the School and Student Unrest: A Theoretical Exploration." In *Uses of the Sociology of Education*, edited by C. Wayne Gordon, National Society for the Study of Education, pp. 36-77. Chicago: University of Chicago Press, 1974.

Udy, Stanley, Jr. "Bureaucracy and Rationality in Weber's Organization Theory: An Empirical Study." *American Sociological Review* 24(1959):791-795.

Udy, Stanley, Jr. "The Comparative Analysis of Organizations." In *Handbook of Organizations,* edited by James March, pp. 678-709. Chicago: Rand McNally, 1965.

White, Orion. "Dialectical Organization: An Alternative to Bureaucracy." *Public Administration Review* 29(1969):32-40.

Willower, Donald; Eidell, Terry; and Hoy, Wayne. *The School and Pupil Control Ideology.* Pennsylvania State University Study No. 24. University Park, Penn., 1967.

Wilson, Bryan. "The Teacher's Role—A Sociological Analysis." *British Journal of Sociology* 13(1962):15-32.

Wilson, James Q. "The Bureaucracy Problem." *The Public Interest* 8(1967):3-9.

Wilson, Woodrow. "The Study of Administration." *Political Science Quarterly* 2(1887):197-222.

Index

Adams, Raymond, 52
Age: of principals, 62-64; of teachers, 11, 92-104
Allison, Graham, 112
Anderson, James, 12-13, 14, 19, 21, 36, 52-54, 55, 56, 65, 72, 93, 101
Atlanta, 7
Authority, 51-52; bureacratic, 52-60; organizational, 65; professional, 65. *See also* Teacher authority

Baltimore City: Department of Education, 22; junior high school teachers, 12-13, 14, 36; public schools, 15, 21-22, 32, 33, 34, 35
Becker, Howard, 18, 28, 62, 78, 88-89
Berman, P., 115
Biddle, Bruce, 79
Bidwell, Charles, 7, 8, 93
Black. *See* Race
Blau, Peter, 52, 64, 71
Bonjean, Charles, 72
Bowles, Samuel, 35

Bowman, Paul, 78
Bureaucracy, 2, 3, 16; defined, 12, 49
Bureaucracy, school, 5, 12-13, 16-19, 112-113; consequences of, 70-91; sources of, 49-69
Bureacracy, street-level, 1, 2-3, 8, 10, 36, 39-40, 72-73
Bureaucratic dysfunctions, 18, 50, 74, 91
Bureaucratic model, 12-13, 15
Bureaucratic organization, 4-5, 50-54, 70-73, 91
Bureaucratic rules, 4-5, 12, 17-19, 52-69, 86, 108, 112-113, 118; and custodial orientation, 73-75; and teacher attitudes, 70-91

Charters, W. W., Jr., 11, 72, 92-93
Classroom routines. *See* Routinization of behavior
Coleman Report, 4, 15, 26, 35
Community control, 5-6, 20, 26, 45-46
Content-oriented teacher, 43, 82